Power up your B2B branding and make your competitors hate you in 35 days

(Starting today)

Rob Dalton

WONDERPUP PRESS
POWER UP YOUR B2B BRANDING AND MAKE YOUR COMPETITORS HATE YOU IN 35 DAYS.
Rob Dalton

Published in the United States by WONDERPUP Press
ISBN: 978-1-54396-918-4

Version 1.1
Printed by BookBaby.

For decades, psychologists have been perpetuating a saying attributed to Eleanor Roosevelt, "No one can make you feel inferior without your consent." This is total B.S. because every time your competitor (you know the one I'm talking about) launches a new ad campaign or marketing stunt, customers eat it up. *Your* customers. Bam! Your heart sinks. Your head explodes. As a marketing professional, you feel you've failed your company. I can only guess but I'll bet your company makes a better product, and your service is far superior, too. (Yup, life isn't fair.) So you have to decide. Will you hang your head and accept defeat? Or worse yet, make excuses for getting beat up on the marketplace playground? Or, is today the day you decide to take charge of your brand and the trajectory of your growth?

If you are a Chief Marketing Officer, Marketing Director, Brand Manager, Digital Marketing Specialist or other influencer of your company's branding and marketing, I want to make you a promise. In 35 days you will stop introducing yourself as the person responsible for your company's marketing, and start introducing yourself as the person IN CHARGE of your company's marketing.

The first several pages of this "how-to" book is a composite transcript of my branding presentations and Messaging Platform workshops. In chapter two, I change gears and talk directly to you.

Not one, but two editors tried to talk me out of writing this book. Because much of its content is heavily biased toward creative- and emotion-driven thinking—stuff both editors felt would unfairly challenge marketing directors and turn off corporate decision-makers. I respectfully disagree. It is not a new concept that people buy on emotion (95% of our brains—and therefore our decisions—are powered by emotion) and later validate their purchase decisions with rational thought. So it is imperative to purposefully create, or re-create your branding and marketing based on emotional expression, not just rational thought and data. I've been using creative- and emotion-based stimuli (you'll see samples later; they look a lot like ads) in my workshops for over 15 years and found that marketing directors and corporate decision makers "get it" and absolutely hone in on how to identify the things that make their brands unique and powerful. And how to articulate their brands' purpose and product features and benefits in unique and powerful ways. To the credit of those editors, the world does not need another how-to-become-a-creative-genius book. If that's your goal, ditch this and buy a copy of Luke Sullivan's book, "Hey Whipple, Squeeze This." Creative stimuli—sample messaging you'll use in brainstorm exercises over the next 35 days—can be easily provided through the relatively inexpensive services of a freelance art director/copywriter team. So don't sweat it; I'll let you know when to consider using outside resources when we get there.

I specialize in Business To Business (B2B) branding and marketing. The information and tips provided in my workshops and in this book primarily apply to B2B brands, but Business to Consumer (B2C) brands will benefit from this information as well. I use the word "branding" to refer to the foundational elements that help prospects identify your company. I use the word "marketing" to refer to the active promotion and generation of interest for your products or services, as well as the creation of an emotional bond between customer and brand. You'll notice I use the words "customer," "consumer" and end-user" interchangeably throughout the book. You'll find more definitions in Chapter Four.

Most of the marketing people I've worked with are ingenious, hard-working and proud of their companies. The problem is, most of them (especially those in B2B) underestimate the power of branding and marketing and rely almost entirely on their sales people and reps to introduce products, build relationships and grow their businesses. My mission is to help them power up their branding and marketing so they can shorten the sales cycle, generate more qualified leads, build stronger customer relationships and leapfrog right over their competitors.

Ad agencies, design firms and public relations companies provide about half of my gigs. To protect these firms, I do not divulge agency names or their clients. In those cases, I've changed or removed company names on the visual examples shown in this book. I have direct relationships with many of the brands I mention and they've given me permission to use their names and show actual examples.

ROB POV

Business to Business marketing is different from Business to Consumer marketing in a nuanced but important way. A typical B2C consumer may buy a coffee mug for herself only to discover the handle gets crazy hot in the microwave. No big deal. The skin on her fingers will grow back and the mug will be exiled to a far corner of her cupboard. But if this same woman buys 1,800 coffee mugs for her company's corporate headquarters (a B2B purchase) only to have 1,800 employees burn their fingers the first time they zap a cup of high-sodium chicken noodle soup, well, that's a much bigger deal. From a dollars and cents perspective, her decision to buy from that brand cost her company a ton of money. But, more importantly, that mug manufacturer made her look incompetent to her boss and her colleagues.

B2B brands MUST provide extensive details about their products and services. B2B marketers MUST take into account the high risks their prospects are making when choosing vendors. B2B marketers MUST truly partner with their customers and always make them look good.

CHAPTER ONE

LET'S START AT THE VERY BEGINNING (A VERY GOOD PLACE TO START)

Marketing and brand management professionals wearing bright blue lanyards mosey into the hotel ballroom two and three at a time. The young ones are excited and chatty as they hustle past my breakout session poster, "Attract customers and grow your business without adding a dime to your marketing budget!" But if you scratch the surface and peek inside their eager, young psyches, you'll find these pups have instantly and involuntarily reconfigured the poster to read, "Learn how to be a marketing genius. Be admired by your colleagues. Get featured in industry magazine articles titled, Rising Star Marketing Whiz Kids to Watch. Quadruple your income!" The seasoned attendees have ridden this rodeo too many times to feel the vibe. By the time they reach 30 the theme tee-shirts, keynote speeches, and "secrets to successful marketing" breakout sessions remind them a little of John Mellencamp's classic lyrics, "Oh yeah, life goes on...long after the thrill of living is gone." But they attend willingly because the conference provides valuable relationship-building opportunities. As the "seniors" walk in and take a seat near the back of the room, they are telepathically muttering to me, "Please, please, please, don't coin a new phrase or bludgeon us with cutesy, motivational, 'refrigerator magnet' sayings."

I am there for the same reasons I wrote his book: to guide the ambitions of the young attendees and to surprise the veterans with branding and marketing advice they didn't expect—stuff they can use tomorrow to shine a light on their brands and kick their competitors' butts. Stuff that will make them better leaders.

At 10:00 o'clock sharp, Julie, the extroverted conference emcee, turns on the mic and her giant smile and with great enthusiasm introduces "Brand therapist" Rob Dalton from Minneapolis, Minnesota. She promises the audience I will delight them with marketing wisdom and turn everything they know about

6

branding and marketing upside down. I love her enthusiasm but Julie is a little off script. I don't want to bring out my inner Larry David, but I'm not there to "delight." I don't spin yarns or tell jokes or "motivate." I'm there because I have something of vital importance to share; a seven word recipe for success. Stand out. Be valuable. Tell the truth. Today's marketers who follow it, succeed. Marketers who don't, don't. Also, I stand before them because I am grateful. I've had a tremendously interesting and satisfying career and I cherish the opportunity to give something back.

Okay, back to Julie's promise I'd turn everything they know about marketing upside-down. The problem is, this audience is already reeling from that very predicament. Over the past few years, it seems everything they knew about marketing had, in fact, been turned upside down. Advertising that successfully attracted prospects in the past, stalled out and stopped working. Calls-to-action led to inaction. New media, digital apps and social channels popped up by the minute—most never getting off the ground—and the majority of those that did flew too close to the sun and vaporized. Almost daily, industry "gurus" are declaring the death of marketing as we know it, offering no viable replacement—only reports about artificial intelligence and machine learning technologies that would soon be replacing human talent, including marketing professionals. The truth is, nearly every marketing professional in the audience is feeling anxious and uncertain and would very much like their worlds repositioned right-side-up.

I clip on my mic, give it an obligatory tap, and begin.

Hello. Everyone in our industry is buzzing about cool advancements in marketing such as the Internet of Things, real-time data collection and predictive analytics, artificial intelligence, machine learning, emerging media and multi-channel experience

7

marketing, and so on. Many of these tools are touted as the holy grail of business growth and profitability. And some may well be for some companies. But not for others. I want your company to successfully leverage the amazing technology platforms and tools available to you. But let's not stop there. I want to change the way you get things done. I want to turn your marketing world to its right-side up position so you have the understanding, confidence, consensus and foundation to make big things happen when you get back to work. Starting tomorrow. And I won't just talk about how "other" brands do it. We're going to explore how YOUR brand will be energized and how YOUR marketing department is going to create a brand foundation and messaging tactics that attract, engage, motivate and retain buyers like never before. The poster outside the door promises I will help you get more from your marketing efforts without spending more money. Let's up the ante. From now on, every tactic you build, from websites, to advertising, to sales materials will be cheaper to create, engage the right prospects and drive more business.

Julie's introduction reminded me of my very first public speaking gig. This will seem like a weird request but are you guys okay if I take a few minutes to talk about that? (A few eyes roll.)

MY FIRST SPEECH

An old high school friend called me in a panic one morning about 10 years ago. He was booked to speak at "Senior Career Day" at Minneapolis Southwest High School. But he was unexpectedly called into a client meeting and pleaded with me to cover for him. The gig was in two hours. I told him I had never given a speech, and had no idea what would interest a bunch of gum-snapping high school seniors. He responded, "They'll think advertising is a cool business so just talk about what you do all day."

8

I reluctantly agreed. Two hours later I stood before a group of about 400 seniors and admitted to them that 35 years earlier I was an unremarkable student at Southwest High School and that I struggled just to graduate. Science, math, history, civics. Man, I barely squeaked by. But my ace-in-the-hole was creative writing and art—subjects that were considered frivolous. And, even though I got good grades, "creative" classes were not the ticket to college in 1973. Neither of my college-educated parents, nor my school counselors even hinted at the idea of exploring colleges. At the ripe old age of 17, my post-high school prospects pointed to a lifetime of minimum-wage jobs.

But listen to this. A few weeks before graduation my English teacher, Sarah Sexton, asked her creative writing class a series of questions that changed the course of my life.

Question 1) Who wishes they could write the next Slaughterhouse Five or Breakfast of Champions? Lots of hands went up.

Question 2) Who thinks it would be cool to usher in a new art movement by painting a Campbell's soup can? More hands went up.

Question 3) Anyone wish they could get rich by directing the next Godfather? More hands shot up.

Question 4) How about getting famous by recording the next After the Gold Rush or Dark Side of the Moon? More hands. My hand went up after every question.

Sarah went on to say that becoming the next Kurt Vonnegut, Andy Warhol, Francis Ford Coppola, Neil Young, et al, was a worthy dream but admittedly, a crazy-difficult long shot. "But," she continued, "What if you didn't have to be the next artistic phenomenon to make a great living doing all the creative things I just talked about?" Now she had our interest. What could it be? "Advertising" said Ms. Sexton. "Advertising is a career where people get paid to create art,

9

music, film and stories. Wow! This was a life-changing moment for me. And by sheer luck, I had just enough talent and samples to secure the last desk available in an advertising graphics program offered at a local technical college.

I spent the next 20 minutes talking about the fun, crazy and satisfying career I'd had, and summed it up with a bit of old man advice. You're 17, maybe 18 years old. You don't need to have your major, or your career, or your entire life figured out right now. Give yourself some time, but pay attention to supportive teachers, coaches and mentors along the way. They may change the course of your life. And when they "gift" you by making a difference, "gift" them back by thanking them and letting them know how they impacted you. As I stand here today I wish I could take my own advice and thank Sarah Sexton. But it's been 35 years and right now she's probably wearing a floppy sun hat, reading a novel on a warm beach in Florida. One of the seniors in the front row raised her pointer finger and quietly said, "Ms. Sexton is upstairs grading papers."

The next few minutes were like a Hallmark Card TV commercial. I tapped on the oak frame of the classroom door. Sarah looked up from her stack of final exams and waved me in. I asked her if she had a minute because something incredible had just happened in the auditorium and she needed to hear about it.

As I introduced myself, she studied my face. I could tell she was mentally photo-shopping out wrinkles and adding to my hairline. I told her she wouldn't remember me because I was kind of an "invisible" student. Then I went on to re-tell the story of that day in her classroom in late May of 1973. And how, for over 35 years, I've written music, created award-winning ad campaigns, art directed TV commercials in Hollywood, collaborated with famous artists and celebrities, all within the context of advertising. And until that fateful day, I had zero prospects for a satisfying career let alone an entire future. I thanked her for a life I could not have dreamed of. Sarah smiled and listened and said nothing. When I finished speaking she put her hands to her face and cried.

I'm going to stop at this point in my story and bring us back to the subject I'm here to talk with you about.

When I asked if I could take a few minutes to talk about the first time I gave a speech, did some of you think to yourself, "Seriously? Why should I listen to this guy blather on about "Career Day," Kurt Vonnegut and Neil Young when I came to learn about branding and marketing?" Your actual response—including the eye rolling—leads to some possible clues about why your current marketing sucks, or at least isn't performing to your expectations.

Let me offer a reality check to make my point. Not one of your prospects woke up this morning hoping to hear about your brand or your products. The story I told you is true and very important to me, but making you wait for the information you came here for was a turn-off and even seemed self-indulgent, right? Even though the story was kind of moving, if you weren't a captive audience, you wouldn't have given me those 4 minutes and 37 seconds to tell it. Think about your website, your advertising and your sales presentations. Are you making your customers wait as you wax on about your brand? Or are you getting right to the stuff they really want to hear?

As long as we're on the subject of prospects who will never become your customers, let's take a brave look at some reasons why.

Reason 1: *They don't need what you have to sell (or at least, they don't need it now). For these people, your marketing is simply irritating background noise.*

Reason 2: *Some people are, well, jerks. A small portion of mankind is cursed with an inflated sense of importance and entitlement. They're the loud phone-talkers. The narcissists. The bullies. The butt-in-liners. They DEMAND the Publix cashier accept a coupon that expired two weeks ago. A coupon for Safeway. Please know, I'm not talking about people who legitimately suffer from mental health issues, addiction or spiritual brokenness. This population deserves our understanding and compassion. But in the context of marketing, you don't need to attract people who, for some weird reason, get satisfaction in being unhappy and nasty to others. If you succeeded, they'd be your worst customers. My favorite terminally disgruntled customer story, as told by business thought leader Alexander Kjerulf, is about a woman who frequently flew the great-price-but-no-frills Southwest Airlines. After each flight she wrote a letter to Southwest's customer relations department complaining about some aspect of her experience. Her last letter included a litany of complaints including the airline's refusal to pre-assign seats, or provide a first class section, or serve in-flight meals. She went on to slam the friendly demeanor of the flight attendants and the casual atmosphere. (Don't you just hate dealing with friendly people?) The letter overwhelmed the customer relations people so they sent it up the ladder to Southwest's CEO Herb Kelleher. In sixty seconds Herb crafted a letter that simply and brilliantly said, Dear Ms. Crabapple, We will miss you. Love, Herb. Take it from Herb, don't compromise your brand values to accommodate jerks.*

Reason 3: *And this one is a biggie. People buy according to their community or "tribal" norms. In broad strokes, tribes are formed and bound by several factors. From a purely marketing perspective; where they live, education level, and income are arguably the most obvious. All of us belong to tribes that share common*

12

rituals, beliefs, values and connections, including connections with brands. Tribal beliefs and perceptions regarding brands may or may not be accurate. But because "belonging" is such a powerful human need, we place more importance on tribal acceptance than in the product itself. Some communities or tribes shun foreign-made motorcycles over American-made. To take it a step further, some tribes insist Harley Davidson is the only acceptable brand of American-made motorcycles. I guarantee there are riders who prefer the look, performance and price of a Victory bike, but the need to comply, and therefore belong to the Harley tribe, transcends their purchase decision.

Successful brands pay attention to tribal connections. Watch any Miller beer TV commercial and you'll see, primarily, men who just finished working with their hands for 10 or 12 hours, enjoying the camaraderie and fermented fruits of their labor. Their tag line is, "It's Miller Time." But the more relevant underlying message is, "If you're an unpretentious, time-clock-punching, hard-working, fun-loving, patriotic American male, "It's Miller TRIBE." A little clunky as a tag line, but you get my drift. Tribes are telling for marketers. The Miller tribe is likely to approve the purchase of a Carhartt jacket and a Ford F-150. If one of their tribe members drove up to the job site in a Lexus, wearing a Arc'teryx jacket they would be judged as haughty—not one of "us."

....

Okay Bub, from this point on I'm no longer reciting a composite of past speeches. I'm talking to YOU, the reader.

— OVERFLOWING SUCCESS —

How a plumbing manufacturer created customer
bonds as strong as their fittings.

Older plumbers favored "tribally-accepted," traditional copper piping over the new, and much easier and faster to install, PEX plastic piping. Uponor, a global manufacturer of PEX piping, used two strategies to sell their products. Strategy "A" was to convert old school plumbers from copper to PEX. Uponor made the transition easy, helping them every step of the way, from specifying, to designing the project, to installing the product. Even though PEX has many tangible benefits over copper, the old schoolers who made the switch to this "new fangled" piping risked acceptance among their tribe members. Strategy "B," Uponor's greater and more sustainable idea, was to create new a tribe of progressive plumbers. They began by identifying contractors and installers who were open to advanced products and technologies.

The plumbing industry is slow to change, but Uponor's marketing strategy is paying off. PEX has become the standard piping for residential applications and is rapidly gaining market share in the commercial space. It isn't just the benefits of PEX piping that caused this growth. It was the satisfaction that came with belonging to a new community of progressive plumbers. "Copper is fine for traditional contractors and installers, but WE are into technology, logic, speed and profitability. WE are Uponor-ites."

Ingrid Mattsson, Uponor's North American Director of Brand and Corporate Social Responsibility doesn't describe Uponor customers as "progressive plumbers." She refers to them as "progressive thinkers."

The original plumbing company, Wirsbo, was founded in Sweden in 1620. (Neither the name *Wirsbo* or the year 1620 are typos.) A few centuries later, a German inventor developed a method to chemically crosslink polyethylene, which led to the invention of PEX piping. For reasons I will not get into, in 2006, the company decided to change their name from Wirsbo to Uponor (go figure). I had the good fortune of being at the right place at the right time to help them with the transition. Wirsbo was always about progress, and in North America, it was also about strong customer relationships. Their culture and their people were passionate, professional and fun.

Announcing a name change. From Wirsbo to weirder.

On January 1, the most trusted name in PEX tubing will become an even more unusual name. What won't change is our commitment to provide the highest quality products and services in the industry.

uponor

uponor.com

This ad, created in 2006, announced a name change while assuring customers two important tenets of the brand —progress and strong relationships—will never change.

This latest ad features Uponor's breakthrough technology. Note the overt expression of progress at the bottom, right corner. The corporate graphics and the products Uponor sells have evolved tremendously since the name change. But the tenets of the brand and the connection with their tribe of progressive thinkers remains steadfast.

Another example of a brand cultivating a tribe is Nike. Back when Nike was an upstart athletic shoe company, they gave hundreds of pairs of shoes to the coolest, most athletic students in high school, and to the coolest, most athletic, winningest sports professionals. In no time, the Nike brand was associated with "real" athletic performance while other shoe brands seemed more concerned with fashion. With this new belief ("WE are all about authentic athletic performance, so WE wear Nikes") a new tribe was born.

Let me share one of my failures to further illustrate my point. A few decades ago I was on a team that created the first ad campaign for a new golf club manufacturer. The brand was owned by one of golf's most famous and respected professional players. The clubs were created using innovative technology and materials. They performed very well. Our ads combined attention-getting headlines and visuals, followed by a scientific explanation of why they performed better that other premium priced clubs. One ad featured a close up photo of a driver with the headline, "Better than steroids. And legal." The body copy described the science behind the proprietary, performance-enhancing design. The ad was a total worm burner. It never took off. It wasn't until I had several more years of experience under my sansabelt that I realized what went wrong. We depended on the power of cleverness to attract prospects' attention, and scientific facts to close the sale. But we never considered the most important consideration: what will happen when our buyers charge onto the first tee box and proudly show off their new, expensive clubs. What happened was nothing. The other players had never heard of this brand and simply shrugged or feigned polite interest. The smart strategy would have been to take a page from Nike's playbook and get the clubs in the hands of famous, winning professional golfers. (Hell, they were personal friends of my client.)

Then, create anticipation for this new brand until a new tribe was created, and *then* run our clever + scientific ads. As I write this book I am consulting with MOOV, an electric-bicycle leasing company. My client's intention was to convert bicycle riders to e-bike riders. By showing prospective customers several messaging options we quickly discovered a tribal barrier. "Real" riders don't ride e-bikes. This led us to a tribe that was not even on our radar screens: commuters. People who found themselves stuck on jammed freeways two times a day were eager to become MOOV e-bike commuters. "WE get to work faster." "WE enjoy the scenery and get exercise along the way." WE are the new MOOV tribe." Our discovery even lead my client to a name change from MOOV, to MOOV Commuter.

Education is tribal, too. High school counselors would be wise to look beyond GPAs, SAT scores and class ranking to include tribal considerations when helping students decide where to go for their post-secondary education. Many high school counselors make the mistake of assuming all students want to "move up" to a more prestigious lot in life so they point them in the direction of the most elite college within academic and financial reach. The truth is, many students would be better served by exploring the continuum of educational opportunities relative to their tribal aspirations. In other words, if a student grew up in a neighborhood comprised of middle-class construction workers, teachers and lab technicians, she may wish to get an education that will lead her to an upper-class tribe comprised of lawyers, doctors and business owners. Then again, she may wish to earn a degree or certificate that will lead to a career within her current tribal norm, a place she already belongs.

If you have a product or service that can be proven superior, but it's just not selling, chances are pretty darn good you're dealing with a tribal barrier. You may get some people to defy their tribes

19

and purchase an "unapproved" product. But the smarter strategy may lie in creating a new tribe your customers can belong to.

ROB POV

It bugs me when people use the word "persuasion" when they describe marketing. My point of view is, marketing should ATTRACT customers, not PERSUADE them. Persuasion is about cajoling or talking someone into doing or buying something. It often relies on discounting…the very strategy that suggests your products or services are over-priced in the first place. Persuasion is a cheap replacement for the hard work that goes into building real trust and value with your customers. Persuasion leads to buyer's remorse and, at best, transactional relationships. Attraction is better. The value of your offerings, the way your brand consistently behaves, the tribes you create, should be self-evident, thus create their own gravitational pull. Loyalty programs should be just that: a gift that is given after the sale, not a tease to get first time trial or to close the sale. If you're thinking, okay, Mr. smarty-pants, why is Groupon such a hit with retail brands? The power lies in the "group" aspect of this phenomenon. Groupon creates mini, short-term tribes. The discount matters, but the rush and hype of membership in a very temporary tribe separates Groupon from coupons.

Here is a marketing phenomenon that can save you money. When a universe of buyers is asked about specific brands, very often about 15% of the respondents will describe themselves as loyal to the brand. They are Honda or Wells Fargo or Costco customers. (I'm using these brands because they all have competitors that provide very similar experiences and products: Honda vs Toyota, Wells Fargo vs Bank of America, and Costco vs Sam's Club.) And conversely, about 15% of the respondents will state NOTHING could convince them to switch brands, even though the competitor's products are very similar, so don't even try, thank you very much.

15%   **15%**

So how does this knowledge help you save money? Your loyal customers (you know who they are) don't need much marketing to keep them happy. Just keep doing what you're doing. The naysayers are unmovable, anyway, so you can stop spending precious marketing dollars to win them over. By not investing in either of these two segments you've just saved 30% of your marketing dollars. But rather than put that money in the bank, I suggest you redirect it toward your biggest marketing opportunity, the 70% in the middle. This huge group is not loyal to any brand. They are open to any brand that makes an emotional connection and meets their rational needs. THIS is the group in which to invest your marketing dollars.

CHAPTER TWO

HOW TO USE THIS BOOK

Leaders, and those who wish to become leaders, know it takes hard work to accomplish significant change. So the first step is to make a commitment to put in the time and effort needed. Step two, roll up your sleeves and let's get started.

A compelling Messaging Platform is the first step to branding and marketing that will be powerful enough to attract customers, drive sales and change the trajectory of your growth.

A Messaging Platform is the foundation or underpinning of all your future sales and marketing communications. It guides all of your internal and external advertising and marketing partners. In just 35 days you and your marketing partners will start creating your website, content, trade show graphics, sales presentations, social media campaigns and advertising with power, clarity and consistency. Additionally, your Messaging Platform establishes a hierarchy of the most important benefits you provide to your customers.

Inside scoop: If you and your team require more than 35 days, so be it. But try not to exceed 56 days. Committing to 35-56 days keeps you and your leadership team engaged and real work gets done. More importantly, you have so much to gain. Why would you want to postpone success?

I've broken the process into 5 weekly sprints. Starting with the next page, your weekly progress will be indicated throughout the remainder of this book.

This interactive process includes several brainstorm sessions. Brainstorming with your colleagues is an energetic and fun experience. After all, the sessions are focused on a company, people and products you are proud of. Here are some general guidelines for

24

preparing and conducting your brainstorm sessions.

• Create an advisory committee that can commit to participating in three brainstorm sessions over the next 35 days. Limit your committee to no more than 12 participants, comprised of your C-suite or top people in marketing, sales, customer support, training, operations, accounting, IT, human resources, R&D and so on. If you feel you must include more than 12 participants, just know that larger groups slow down the sessions a bit and require a little extra work to keep everyone engaged. If you are a small company or a startup with as few as one stakeholder, invite some trusted and smart business professionals to join your advisory committee. The brainstorm sessions provide great results with as few as four participants so don't sweat it if you have limited human resources available to you.

Inside Scoop: In my practice, I've compensated outside participants for their time, but more often asked for "free" advice and then rewarded each of them a gift card from a local restaurant or coffee shop at the conclusion of the sessions.

• Conduct your brainstorm sessions off-site if possible, and insist mobile devices are not invited. The sessions get intense and you'll get the best input if your participants are focused and uninterrupted. Some of the sessions include breakout exercises so a large room with access to a few smaller rooms is ideal.

• I've prescribed time parameters for each brainstorm session. Brainstorming at a fast pace keeps the energy and ideas flowing. If you find your group is more comfortable or productive working at a slower pace, adjust the duration times at your discretion.

• Materials and equipment needed for brainstorm sessions:

– White Board or poster-size Post-it pad

– Color printer that can print 11x17 sheets

1------------------ 2 ------------------ 3 ------------------ 4 ------------------ 5

– Roll of blue, low-adhesive painter's tape

– Pens and note paper or Post-it pads for each participant

– Large marker for facilitator

– Small round paper stickers, about the size of a quarter. (Available at any office supply store.) Before Session 2—Your Biggest, Most Important Brainstorm Session—cut the pages containing round stickers into strips of six. You'll need two strips of six stickers for each participant.

– Chocolate chip cookies

FREE DOWNLOADABLE TOOLKIT

Many of the worksheets and templates I refer to in this book are available in my free Toolkit. Download the Toolkit at daltonbrandcatalyst.com using the (all caps) password: WONDERPUP

CHAPTER THREE

WISHFUL THINKING WILL GET YOU EVERYWHERE

In this chapter we'll kick into gear and start developing your brand's Messaging Platform. We'll cover how to facilitate discovery interviews (which you will conduct in week two) and your first brainstorm session, *Wishes and Barriers*.

The discovery interviews, along with brainstorm session one, will help you hone in on your specific needs and the solutions that will help you power up your branding and marketing. I want to discuss the discovery interview process now in week one because, in order to have participants chat within week two, you'll need to send them a Request For Interview now. The discovery interviews have two functions:1) To get an overview on how your leadership, employees and customers perceive the brand...what's working, what's not, and what language they use to articulate their perceptions. 2) To give every key internal stakeholder an opportunity to be heard, which is a critical step in reaching a group consensus.

• Start your discovery interviews by creating a list of 6-10 INTERNAL participants. Internal participants should be a mix of leaders from various departments such as operations, management, manufacturing, marketing, HR, IT, sales, and so on. Ideally, your list should include both long standing and relatively new employees. Your long standing participants have deep knowledge of your brand and its culture. Your newer employees will easily remember what attracted them to your company or organization.

• Next, create a list of 10-15 EXTERNAL participants. Ultimately, you'll want to conduct 6-10 external interviews. Based on my experience, many of the people you contact will be unwilling or unavailable to be interviewed, so ask about 30% more people than you actually need. These participants should be comprised of new customers who can easily recall why they were attracted to your brand, and long standing-customers who will have a deeper relationship and understanding of your brand.

• When scheduling your interviews, allow one interview per 45 minute chunk of time. Your internal participants are likely to talk longer than 30 minutes. Many of your external interview participants will answer your questions in 2 and 3 syllable answers. Gently prod them for more. Most of your external interviews will be wrapped up within 20 minutes.

• Send an email Request For Interview to both internal and external participants. A sample is on the following page. Feel free to re-write your Request For Interview in your own voice.

• Your goal is to conduct the interviews in week two. Once a date and time is set, send each participant a calender invite.

SUBJECT LINE: We're making improvements starting with you.
EMAIL:

Dear (customer name),

Since we opened our doors in (year) we've been constantly delighted and grateful for the team we've assembled, for our success, and for the relationships we've built. As we look to the future, we are carefully examining every aspect of our business in order to stay the course of our growth goals, and to better meet the needs of our customers. I'm writing you today to ask for your help. I would like to conduct a 30 minute, one-on-one phone interview at your convenience sometime during the week of (date). I'll ask you about your experiences with our company...what you feel worked well and what we could improve upon. If you're agreeable and available, send me one or two day/time options for the phone call. Please include the phone number where I can reach you and I'll initiate the call. Your opinions are valuable to us. Thanks in advance for your help!

Respectfully yours,
(Name)

This Request For Interview template is best for existing companies or organizations. This along with a version for start-up companies or organizations is available in the Toolkit at daltonbrandcatalyst.com.

FACILITATING THE INTERVIEWS

• Start each interview by thanking your participant and reminding them how important their honest input is to the future of your company.

• Use the interview questions shown on the following page. (Included in the Toolkit.) While they should be fairly easy to answer, they give you an opening to go deeper, which many participants will happily oblige. By the way, if you choose to send the questions ahead of the interview, please know many of your participants will not look at it before your interview. I typically do not send the questions ahead of the interviews.

• Allow your participants to talk as long as they wish. Well, to a point. Near the end of the interview there are two questions focused, not on your brand, but on the participants themselves. By the time you get the those questions, your participants are warmed up and eager to tell you what they like and dislike about their jobs, and how your brand affects their challenges, solutions, frustrations and joy.

• Thank them for their time and input.

Inside Scoop: Your participants are sharing their beliefs and perceptions. And they may not be true, accurate, or consistent with your beliefs and perceptions. Don't correct them during the interview, because that could derail the momentum.

• In my practice I aggregate the answers on a spreadsheet and use this as a cheat sheet for creating sample messaging and other stimuli for future brainstorm sessions. More on that later.

Next up, brainstorm session one, *Wishes and Barriers.*

DALTON BRAND CATALYST

BRAND STRATEGY QUESTIONNAIRE

NAME _____

How long have you had a relationship with (company)?

What are 2-3 key words that describe (company)?

What 2-3 things does (company) do well? -or- What problem does (company) solve?

What is the best kept secret about (company)? (Something you might not know about until you have an interaction.)

What's unique about (company) or its offerings?

What could (company) do differently or better?

(FOR INTERNAL STAKEHOLDERS) What could (company) do differently or better relative to marketing?

Is there anything the competition does that you wish (company) could do?

What do you feel are the reasons (company) employees show up for work other than a paycheck?

Has anything in the marketplace changed that might cause someone to consider switching to (company)?

What is the best part of your job?

What is your least favorite part of your job?

If I handed you a megaphone and asked you to make one bold statement about why a prospect (or the world) should pay attention to (company), what would that be?

This is a GENERAL Interview template for use by established companies and organizations.

DALTON BRAND CATALYST

STARTUP BRAND STRATEGY QUESTIONNAIRE

NAME _____

Step One: Prepare a 250 words or fewer description of your company and its products and services. Include a brief description of your target audience, e.g., Professionals who are responsible for purchasing cleaning products and equipment for their enterprise.

Step Two: Start your interview by thanking your participant. Explain that you are looking for feedback that may help you introduce this new company to the world, and that their honest feedback is valuable and appreciated. Read your company description and ask if there are any questions before you launch into the interview.

Step Three: The questions.

AS DESCRIBED...

1) Is the concept for this company and its products and/or services understandable?

2) Do you feel the concept for this company and its products and/or services is unique?

3) Do you feel the features and benefits as I described them are believable?

4) What do you find most appealing or intriguing about this company and its offerings?

5) What do you find least appealing or intriguing about this company and its offerings?

6) Do you feel the target audience I described will have a positive response to this company and its offerings?

7) Do you feel others who do not fit this profile would be interested in this company and its offerings?

8) If you were suddenly the spokesperson for this new startup, what sentence or two would you "yell from the mountaintop" to get the attention of the people we wish to attract?

This is a STARTUP Interview template. I have not talked about this but it's most useful for new companies. Both are available in the Toolkit.

Welcome to Week Two!

BRAINSTORM SESSION ONE

PART ONE—WISH LIST

OBJECTIVE: For you and your marketing department to understand the most important needs and opportunities in which marketing could play a role.

TOTAL SESSION TIME: 90 Minutes. PART ONE: 45 Minutes.

DIRECTIONS: Your advisory committee will generate, discuss and prioritize specific things they wish marketing would or could accomplish for your company.

• Start by posting the statement on a white board, "I wish our marketing would help us _____
because_____".

• Hand out individual sheets (available in the Toolkit) and ask each participant to complete the sentence. Suggest they try for at least 6 or 7 "wishes."

• Give them 15 minutes to do this. Announce when their time is up.

Inside scoop: Participants are likely to list tactics like, "I wish we had a sales brochure because prospects ask for them." To help them understand you are looking for goal-centric, big impact wishes, give them an example such as, "I wish our marketing would attract younger buyers because many of our current customers will be retiring soon."

1--------------2--------------3--------------4--------------5

DALTON BRAND CATALYST | WISHES

NAME _____

I WISH our marketing would help us _____

because _____

I WISH our marketing would help us _____

because _____

I WISH our marketing would help us _____

because _____

I WISH our marketing would help us _____

because _____

I WISH our marketing would help us _____

because _____

I WISH our marketing would help us _____

because _____

I WISH our marketing would help us _____

because _____

A WISHES Template is included in the Toolkit.

1 -------------- 2 -------------- 3 -------------- 4 -------------- 5

Here is a partial list of marketing wishes I've collected from past brainstorm sessions.

I WISH our marketing would...

- BUILD AWARENESS because OUR MARKETING IS OVERSHADOWED BY OUR COMPETITORS.
- HELP PROSPECTS SELF SELECT because OUR SALES TEAM IS CHASING EVERYONE WHO HAS A PULSE.
- ATTRACT YOUNGER CUSTOMERS because OUR OLDER CUSTOMERS ARE AGING OUT.
- DEMONSTRATE WHAT MAKES US BETTER because WE HAVE GREAT PRODUCTS THAT SPEAK FOR THEMSELVES.
- EXPAND INTO NEW MARKETS because WE ARE SCALABLE.
- TAKE ADVANTAGE OF NEW MARKETING TECHNOLOGIES because WE CAN REACH THE RIGHT PEOPLE AT A LOWER COST.
- RETAIN CUSTOMERS because WE'RE LOSING THEM TO NEW, UNPROVEN COMPETITORS.
- LAUNCH (SPECIFIC) INITIATIVE because IT'S PART OF OUR GROWTH STRATEGY.
- INCLUDE EDUCATIONAL AND TRAINING CONTENT because OUR CUSTOMERS VALUE THIS.
- FEND OFF OUR COMPETITION because THEY ARE STEALING MARKET SHARE FROM US.
- REPAIR OUR REPUTATION because WE'VE FIXED THE PROBLEM.
- ENHANCE THE CUSTOMER EXPERIENCE because CUSTOMER EXPECTATIONS HAVE GROWN.
- TURN OUR EMPLOYEES INTO BRAND ADVOCATES because THEY CAN BE OUR MOST EFFECTIVE SALES FORCE.
- ALL I KNOW IS OUR WEBSITE SUCKS AND WE DON'T KNOW WHAT TO DO ABOUT IT because WELL, THAT'S ALL I KNOW.

• For the next 20 minutes, ask individuals to select their top three wishes and take turns reading them aloud. Post them on a white board as they are read. (Assure the group you will collect all of their wishes at the end of the session for future consideration.)

• There will probably be lots of duplication so ask advisory members to avoid answers that have already been listed.

• Read your three top wishes aloud to the group.

• Congratulate the group for generating exciting and innovative wishes, and for the remaining 10 minutes, ask the group to help you prioritize the top five AS IF MONEY WERE NOT AN OBJECT. This may be chaotic and you may not reach absolute conclusions but remind them this exercise is designed to understand what they feel would help the company compete and grow.

Inside scoop: If you've presented marketing initiatives or campaign ideas to leadership only to be shut down, this approach changes everything for two reasons: Reason One: Leadership was involved in the creation of the wishes, so they have ownership in them. Reason Two: The top wishes you are pursuing have been virtually preapproved by all key stakeholders.

I've found most company principles are capable of establishing the foundational tenets of their brands—Mission, Vision and Values—with minimal input from consultants or business books. In past "wishes" exercises, the creation of guiding principals rarely make the wish list. A somewhat greater challenge is identifying qualified prospects and reaching them exactly when they are open to considering a different brand. But these issues don't often appear on the wish list either, because better and cheaper technologies are helping marketers accomplish this. In my practice, the majority of wish list entries have to do with business-driving marketing initiatives such as improving the customer experience or breaking into a new category. These initiatives often identify the need for new or improved marketing tactics. That said, most of this book focuses on how to create a Messaging Platform that will address "must win" initiatives and help you create tactics better, faster and cheaper than ever before.

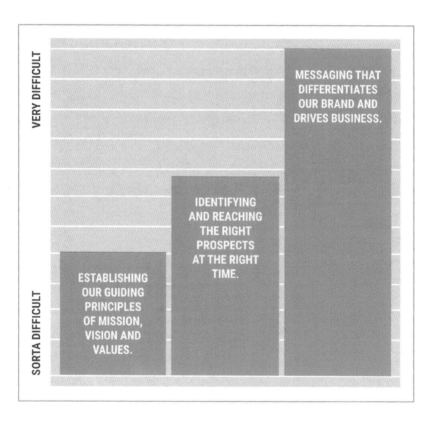

BRAINSTORM SESSION ONE
PART TWO—BARRIERS

OBJECTIVE: For you and your advisory committee to understand the most critical barriers to becoming better, more effective marketers.

PART TWO TIME: 45 Minutes.

DIRECTIONS: Over the next 45 minutes, your advisory committee will generate and discuss specific barriers they feel are currently or potentially keeping your company from achieving the things on your marketing wish list.

• Start by posting the statement, "A barrier that prevents us from achieving our marketing wishes is_____" and ask them to individually complete the sentence on a sheet of paper (available in the Toolkit).

• Give them 15 minutes to do this. Announce when their time is up. A sampling of barriers is listed on the following pages.

• Generate your list of barriers, too.

• Just as you did with the marketing "wishes" portion of the brainstorm session, for the next 20 minutes, ask individuals to select their top 3 barriers and take turns reading them aloud to the group. Post them on a white board as they are read. (Assure the group you will collect all of their wishes at the end of the session for future consideration.)

• Again, there will probably be lots of duplication and you may only get a handful of unique barriers. When duplicates occur, just place a check mark next to the original entry. If you feel you need more barriers, ask each participant to call out a barrier not already listed.

• If your group generates tons of barriers, take a few extra minutes and separate them into four marketing related buckets: PEOPLE BARRIERS (such as lack of awareness or vision or skills), PROCESS BARRIERS (lack of analysis, planning, financial support, technology, coordination between sales and marketing), POSITIONING BARRIERS (lack of clarity regarding what we do, how we do it better, why we matter to the world), and "OTHER" BARRIERS (a catchall).

• For the remaining 10 minutes of your brainstorm session, ask the group to help you prioritize the top five barriers AS IF MONEY WERE NOT AN OBJECT. This may be chaotic and you may not reach absolute conclusions but remind them this exercise is designed to get a sense of what barriers they feel are hindering your marketing and the growth of your company.

Asking for participation and getting consensus on key marketing barriers will greatly improve your ability to get approval, funding and support to move forward on improving your branding and marketing.

Inside scoop: In both exercises, your participants prioritized Wishes and Barriers as if money were not an object. This direction opens up their thinking and keeps them from editing their own ideas. Later, your job is to select Wishes and Barriers that will provide impact toward the growth of your brand within the confines of your marketing budgets. BTW, having leadership involved in this exercise may result in bigger marketing budgets!

NAME _____

A BARRIER that prevents us from achieving our marketing WISHES is _____

_____

A BARRIER that prevents us from achieving our marketing WISHES is _____

_____

A BARRIER that prevents us from achieving our marketing WISHES is _____

_____

A BARRIER that prevents us from achieving our marketing WISHES is _____

_____

A BARRIER that prevents us from achieving our marketing WISHES is _____

_____

A BARRIER that prevents us from achieving our marketing WISHES is _____

_____

A BARRIER that prevents us from achieving our marketing WISHES is _____

_____

A BARRIERS Template is included in the Toolkit.

1------------------ 2 ------------------ 3 ------------------ 4 ------------------ 5

Here is a partial list of marketing barriers I've collected from past brainstorm sessions.

BARRIERS that prevent us from achieving our marketing wishes are...
- INSUFFICIENT MARKETING BUDGET.
- CONFUSION—OUR BRAND MEANS 10 DIFFERENT THINGS TO 10 DIFFERENT EMPLOYEES (NOT TO MENTION OUR CUSTOMERS).
- OUR COMPETITORS OUTSPEND US. BY A LOT.
- OUR MESSAGING DOESN'T PERFORM WELL IN DIGITAL CHANNELS.
- WE ADVERTISE, BUT WE DON'T KNOW IF IT'S WORKING.
- WE CAN'T GET LEADERSHIP TO AGREE ON BUSINESS OBJECTIVES OR A MARKETING STRATEGY.
- THERE'S NO SIGNIFICANT DIFFERENCE BETWEEN US AND OUR COMPETITION, SO...
- WE'RE TOO BUSY TO TRY NEW MARKETING APPROACHES.
- WE HAVE NO MARKETING PROCESSES IN PLACE.
- NO ONE SEES AND/OR BELIEVES ADVERTISING ANYMORE.
- DIGITAL MARKETING CHANGES SO FAST WE DON'T KNOW WHERE TO START.
- WE HAD AN AD AGENCY ONCE, BUT THEY JUST DIDN'T "GET" OUR BRAND AND THEY COST WAAAAY TOO MUCH.
- THE BOSS'S IDIOT NEPHEW BUILT OUR CRAPPY WEBSITE BUT NO ONE DARES TO CRITICIZE IT.
- OUR SALES AND MARKETING DEPARTMENTS DON'T TALK TO EACH OTHER SO OUR EFFORTS ARE WASTED AND OUR MESSAGING IS INCONSISTENT.
- WE DON'T HAVE THE APPROPRIATE TALENT ON BOARD.
- SOME OF US DON'T BELIEVE IN MARKETING.

Here's a sample of one company's top three Wishes and Barriers.

WE WISH OUR MARKETING WOULD HELP US...
- Attract a younger audience
- Differentiate our brand from our competitors
- Provide a better customer experience

BARRIERS WE FEEL ARE PREVENTING US FROM
ACHIEVING OUR MARKETING WISHES ARE...
- Not enough money allocated to support our marketing goals
- We don't know what's important to younger prospects
- Our marketing and advertising approval process sucks so
tactics tend to run out of steam and never get done.

Congratulations! By reaching a consensus on your marketing wishes and barriers, (most marketing professionals and their companies never achieve this, but YOU have) you are on your way to a marketing plan that will grow your business. By involving leadership and your advisory committee, you've also created an appetite for more effective marketing.

Cue the science-fiction music. Call it a coincidence, a God thing, Karma, or the Quantum Theory of Phase Entanglement, but having your specific wishes and barriers in mind as you continue to use this book will create a gravitational pull towards the solutions and ideas most relevant to your needs. It sounds kind of spacey but WHAT YOU NEED MOST WILL JUMP OFF THE PAGES.

ROB POV

WHY THREE?

I create clumps of three. A lot. Choose your top three wishes. Choose your top three barriers. The recipe for success includes three ingredients. I wish I could continue the theme and give you three reasons why I do this, but there are just two. The first of which is, human beings can retain and deal with three related pieces of information far better than four or five. You may have identified a dozen things that differentiate your brand, but your prospects will hang with you long enough to learn, believe, remember and share three. Many of your prospects will be recommending your brand "upstream" without you in the room, so limiting your unique attributes to three makes it easy for them to explain to decision makers why they want to partner with your brand.

Secondly, three initiatives are manageable. Emotionally if not financially. If your Marketing Wish List had 20 entries, your team is likely to scratch the surface on many but accomplish little.

How is it that a wimpy, little four-legged stool keeps lions from devouring their tamers? When they see all four legs coming at them all at once, lions become confused and paralyzed. Too many choices turns them into pussycats and they go after none.

CHAPTER FOUR

ZAMPO OV SLEGER BLANERBOM

Let's talk about words. When you use marketing-speak with your stakeholders, the title of this chapter is exactly what you sound like. Many of the problems that lurk behind weak brand foundations and ineffective marketing start with inconsistent language and confusing industry jargon. In order to move forward, you and your stakeholders must discuss and agree upon the basic tenets of your brand. Deep-dive stuff like your brands' Mission, Vision, and Values. This exercise can be chaotic if everyone on your marketing team uses different words for the same concepts. I use the word "MISSION" to describe why a brand exists. But members of your team may use terms like "PASSION STATEMENT," "PURPOSE," TRUE NORTH," "MOUNTAINTOP," "ESSENTIAL TRUTH," "CORE FOCUS," "WHY," and others for the exact same thing.

If discussing branding and marketing with your corporate decision makers leads to moderate-to-severe confusion and shortness of patience, this glossary of terms can help enlighten your team and get everyone on the same page.

ADVERTISING

A subset of your MARKETING mix: typically paid media tactics and channels including television, radio, newspaper/magazine ads, outdoor boards, transit posters, social media/digital ads, "advertorials," brochures and direct mail.

BRAND

A brand is the source of a product or service. Its primary function is to establish trust between the manufacturer or retailer and the customer/consumer/end user.

BRANDING

Assigning a name, logo, colors, type fonts and foundational tenets such as VISION, MISSION, and VALUES that help buyers identify your products or services from others. Branding also includes the organization's history, reputation and promise it makes to its customers.

BRAND VISION

What we want to become.

Amazon's Vision Statement: To be the earth's most customer-centric company; to build a place where people can come to find and discover anything they might want to buy online.

BRAND MISSION

Why we exist.

Caterpillar's Mission Statement: To enable economic growth through infrastructure and energy development, and to provide solutions that support communities and protect the planet.

By the way, Mission Statements don't have to be poetic or fanciful. DataDog's mission statement: To bring sanity to IT Management.

BRAND VALUES

What we believe in and how we will behave, especially when something goes wrong. Dalton Brand Catalyst's brand values are Integrity, Collaboration, and Responsiveness.

BRAND PROMISE

This is an outward-facing promise you make to the world. It is the solution to your customers' and prospects' problem that no other brand can provide. (At least not as well as your brand can.)

BRAND STORY

This is a narrative that explains where the company is located, who you serve, what problems you solve, how you solve them and what drives your employees. And finally, how you want your customers to feel because they choose to partner with, or buy from, you.

MARKETING

The action of promoting and generating interest in your brand and its products and services. This is done through market research, SEO, pricing, promotions, advertising, websites, packaging, point of purchase displays, product placement, on-line ads, social media, direct mail, email, public relations, "guerilla" tactics, word-of-mouth, trade shows, events, immersive experiences, radio, newspaper and magazine ads, outdoor boards, transit posters, social media, digital ads, "advertorials," brochures and direct mail.

MARKETING STRATEGY

The three elements that make up your Marketing Strategy are your Objective (what you intend to achieve within a particular time frame), your Value Proposition (your brand's unique products, services and expertise that solve your customers' problems), and your Scope (how and where you are going to deliver on your Value Proposition.)

MARKETING OBJECTIVES

These tend to be long-term, broad-based initiatives that lead to specific measurable goals. Examples: Increase brand awareness SO THAT (goal goes here) we can shorten the sales cycle. Grow our digital presence SO THAT (goal goes here) we can reach a younger audience. Simplify our website SO THAT (goal goes here) customers have a better shopping experience.

MARKETING GOALS

These tend to be measurable results your company wishes to achieve from a specific promotion or marketing strategy within a set period of time. Examples: Increase sales 20% in 24 months. Add 10 new accounts to our roster in 12 months. Attract 250 more prospects to next year's trade show.

MESSAGING PLATFORM

Sometimes called a Communications Guide, this is a crystallization and hierarchy of key customer benefits and brand differentiators. The Messaging Platform serves as an underpinning for all sales, marketing and advertising communications, starting with a captivating Brand Promise (a solution your brand provides). The Brand Promise is supported by three Support Pillars that, when combined, separate your brand from all others. Under each Support Pillar are Talking Points: proof, facts or supportive statements that hold up the Pillar and further unite the brand with your audiences.

VALUE PROPOSITION

This is an inward-facing declaration about your brand's unique ability to provide benefits, solutions and value to your customers and prospects. It's "what we do," "How we do it better," and "Why we matter to the world." (Note: The *outward*-facing declaration is your BRAND PROMISE.)

You may decide to continue using the marketing words or phrases your team is comfortable with and that's fine. But be consistent. If you feel the term "True North" is a better term than "Brand Mission" for *why we exist* just make sure everyone on your team uses that term every time.

There are hundreds of other marketing terms, acronyms and buzz words. But keeping language basic, simple and consistent is the first step in building your improved branding and messaging platform.

ROB POV

BRAND PROMISE VS. VALUE PROPOSITION

Value Propositions (aka, Unique Selling Points) are about your brand and the stuff your brand is uniquely qualified to offer. Nearly every brand I've worked with has struggled to craft a Value Proposition that resonates with internal as well as external audiences. The way I see it, VALUE PROPOSITIONS ARE AN INTERNAL DECLARATION, useful for behind-the-curtain discussions, marketing strategy development, and occasional pats on the back. A BRAND PROMISE IS ABOUT WHAT YOUR CUSTOMERS GET FOR ENGAGING WITH YOUR BRAND. I think that's better. Your prospects and customers will only listen to stuff about your brand for so long. What they're waiting for is how your brand will solve THEIR problems and how your products will improve THEIR lives. A Brand Promise is your external declaration that gets to the heart of what matters to them.

CHAPTER FIVE

YOUR RECIPE
FOR MARKETING SUCCESS:
STAND OUT
BE VALUABLE
TELL THE TRUTH

There are few hard and fast rules in marketing. At least rules worth following. But I believe following these three rules is critical to the long-term success of any company or organization.

STAND OUT. BE VALUABLE. TELL THE TRUTH.

Let me unpack them, last to first.

TELL THE TRUTH. Building trust between your brand and your customers is the single most important job of marketing. It's about consistently doing the "right thing" and understanding it takes a long time to earn trust and a few minutes to destroy it. Today more than ever we live in a climate of "alternative facts," rigged outcomes, misleading claims, hidden costs, and unacceptable corporate behavior. Lack of trust can manifest in many ways, all of which cost companies money. Today, Facebook, Wells Fargo, UBER, VW, and a slew of other companies are feeling the backlash of their deceptive practices and lies. Many of these companies are running advertising campaigns asking for their customers for forgiveness. Why? Because customers leave. In July of 2018, when the public was made aware of Facebook's mishandling (make that SELLING) of personal data, the company lost over $100 billion in one day as its stock nose-dived 19 percent. That's the biggest single day loss in stock market history. Opinion polls found that fewer than half of Americans trust Facebook to obey U.S. privacy laws. Facebook and other social media giants have been burying information about how the company handles their customers' personal data in many, many, many pages of fine print. But wait, there are other ways marketers destroy trust.

Click-bait. A few months ago I got an AT&T "alert" text stating my account had been altered and I should go online immediately to see how this impacts me. I stopped whatever I was doing, certain my phone had been hacked, only to read the message, "CONGRATULATIONS! You're eligible for a $10 discount on Direct TV for six months when you bundle your phone and TV services!" This deceiving marketing sent me from trusting AT&T to distrusting them in 60 seconds. Plumbing companies to airlines have been known to artificially widen the definition of "on-time" just to claim superior punctual service.

Premium clothing brands sell their stuff at outlet malls for less. What many fail to tell their unsuspecting buyers is that these garments and accessories were made specifically for sale at outlet malls, at a lower quality.

Snack companies have been busted for retaining their prices while quietly reducing the amount of food in the package. You've probably noticed a brand or two that replaced a few cookies with bigger cardboard spacers so the package retains its normal size.

Some companies lie by omission. When a phone carrier lowered its monthly rates to entice new customers, they instructed their ad agency to create an email campaign to trick current customers into renewing their contracts at the older, higher rate.

Deceiving practices, unethical behavior and lies eventually get found out. And because of social media, the news spreads quickly. The result? Trust in media, government, organized religion and corporations is at an all-time low. However, this creates an opportunity to set your brand apart by exercising truth and transparency in your marketing and in the way you conduct your business. Later in this book you'll explore possible messaging styles for your brand. Be sure to pay attention to headlines and statements that include hyperbole and exaggerated claims. They're the gateway to trouble.

1------------- 2 ------------- 3 ------------- 4 ------------- 5

BE VALUABLE. If your marketing is not valuable, it's just background noise. Of course, being "valuable" means providing great products and services. But today, every interaction between brand and customer or prospect must bring a level of value in order to advance your brand and grow your business. Marketing with a capital "M" is about how your customers EXPERIENCE your brand, from website or in-store visits to using your products to registering a complaint. Capital "M" marketing always delivers value. Small "m" marketing includes advertising and other paid media, often void of significant value. Nordstrom expresses marketing with a capital "M" through exceptional service. They don't run ads about great service, they provide it, every day. And their customers love it and talk about it. Hmmm, I wonder if that's why Macy's, Sears and JCPenny are closing stores while Nordstrom is building them?

I've worked with medical clinic marketing directors who get wrapped around the axle because, while they're expected to grow the business, medical marketing is closely regulated, leaving them no opportunity to make claims that differentiate their clinic or products from their competitors. On top of that, their doctors feel the value of the brand is based 100% on patient outcomes, leaving no place (and not a lot of respect) for marketing.

Here's something to ponder. On average, a patient will be in a clinic for 47 minutes. She'll be with her doctor for about 12 of those minutes. So, how can you deliver marketing value during those other 35 minutes? Let's say your clinic specializes in geriatric care. And your Brand Promise is ease-of-use for older patients. What would be more valuable to your patient, a magazine ad that talks about how much your clinic cares about older patients? Or a cool, new check-in procedure that, instead of standing in line, patients can take a seat and a tablet-in-hand concierge will *come to them* to check them in and get the necessary information? Oh, and provide a hot cup of coffee, too. That's marketing value. Will an 88-year-old patient jump on social media and wax rhapsodic about her wonderful check-in experience? Probably not. But her daughter will.

A building materials company I recently worked with knew how stressful final construction walkthroughs are for general contractors. At that point in time, occupants are physically and emotionally ready to move in and any delay could cause a series of problems, complaints and misgivings about his company. My client developed an app that guided the contractor through the inspection and allowed him to confirm and record every item that was move-in ready, and items that still needed attention, such as a cracked bathroom tile. But the app did one more trick. It automatically ordered the new part in real time, so installers could replace it hours if not days sooner than the traditional method. So, what do you think is the most valuable marketing tool in their sales meetings, their slick brochures or that cool app?

STAND OUT. Most marketing fails simply because it's not noticed or it's not emotionally compelling. Marketing and advertising professionals intuitively know how to get people to notice their messaging. The problem is, sometimes they use emotional triggers that command attention but don't reflect the personality and values of the brand. Ad agencies can be guilty of creating messaging that reflects *their* brand instead of their clients' brands. Choosing an inappropriate emotional trigger is what lurks behind the statement, "I don't know exactly why I can't approve this campaign/website/sales presentation/etc. It just doesn't feel right." The solution is to bring logic, process and options to the table *before* creating marketing tactics. Inviting your stakeholders and decision makers to explore various emotional triggers leads to messaging that stands out, creates an emotional connection *and* reflects your brand. This collaborative approach also leads to a big, honkin' benefit besides standing out. It leads to consensus. Getting stakeholder and leadership consensus on the emotional triggers that will attract prospects' attention and align with your brand values will pay huge dividends and accelerate the creation of your marketing and advertising tactics. We'll be discussing how to create stimuli and facilitate an emotional triggers exploration later in this book.

To be clear, ther vast majority of today's advertising: 1) Doesn't get noticed. 2) Doesn't motivate buyers. 3) Doesn't get talked about. You need all three.

Branding is about helping people connect products and promises with the company of origin. Marketing that stands out with emotion, personality and value leads to attraction, engagement, and brand preference.

There are dozens of U.S. companies that manufacture and sell kitchen cabinets to single- and multi-family home builders. In the home page example on the following page, the premium quality and beauty of the cabinets provide the emotional kick needed to attract and hold a home builder's attention. (Please note I've removed the manufacturer's logo.) After all, "PREMIUM" is a key selling point for builders when they are pitching their customers; the potential home buyers.

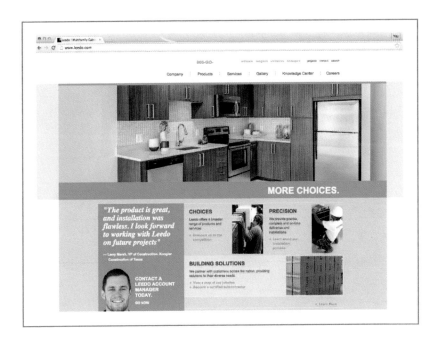

But look what happens when a competitor also uses "premium" quality and beauty as a means of attracting a prospect.

And another.

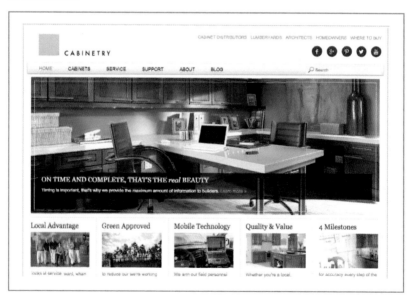

And another.

And another.

A "sea of sameness" occurs when smaller manufacturers emulate industry leaders. (In website as well as product development.) Eventually, no one stands out. The playing field is leveled and prospects are confused.

If you live in Minnesota, there's a good chance you went to school with someone named Ron Anderson. Or you currently work with someone named Ron Anderson. Or you *are* Ron Anderson. The Ron Anderson I'm talking about was a uniquely gifted ad executive who could out-present Don Draper. His advertising agency was pitching a luxury car account and Ron decided to demonstrate how virtually every car company was using a captivating-but-similar formula to entice buyers. The conference room lights dimmed as Ron hit the play button on the VCR. Ron's prospects sat through five 30-second TV spots, all from different car makers. Each opened on a close-up shot of the car, then cut to an overhead curvy mountain road, then to a quick scene of the driver lovingly caressing the leather. A few more seconds in, the car makes its way down a bustling city street, cut to a two-second head-turn of an admiring (and beautiful) pedestrian...and finally a tail-lights-into-the-sunset closing scene with the car makers' logo superimposed. To drive (pun intended) home his point, Ron had swapped out all of the sound tracks so they played against a competitor's film. In other words, the voice and music for BMW played over the Lexus film, and so on. Amazingly, the scripts, music and film synced up perfectly regardless of the combination. Ron made his point without saying a word.

Let me repeat my point. Branding is about helping people find you and connect your products with your company. Marketing that stands out is about using emotion, personality and value to rise above your competition.

1 --------------- 2 --------------- 3 --------------- 4 --------------- 5

B2B marketing doesn't need to go overboard to stand out. Overstating (yelling) your message probably won't reflect who you are as a brand. So, how different should your branding and marketing be in order to stand out from the crowd? There's an old riddle that can help me answer this question.

A giant grizzly bear wanders onto a campsite. Immediately, dozens of startled campers run for their lives. Q: To save your skin, do you have to outrun the bear? A: Nope, you just have to outrun the slowest camper. You see, your website (and other marketing) doesn't have to be twice as captivating as every other website out there, just a little better than your competitors'. A rule of thumb—be 20% more compelling than your competition.

The example above demonstrates the 20% rule. Like the other manufacturers, this home page highlights the beauty of the product. But the design is cleaner and the headline is more inviting, invoking a smile. Rather than blathering about themselves, this home page addresses the three most important needs of the manufacturer's prospects and customers (home builders): products that are on-trend, priced right, and delivered on time. This example works equally as well under the "Be Valuable" rule. A video about cabinet styles and color trends is a valuable feature to home builders. So are the videos with tips on how to stay on budget and keep projects on schedule. This example stands out just a little more than the others. Check out your competitors' home pages. If it's a sea-of-sameness, you've got a huge opportunity ahead of you.

ROB POV

SALES VS. MARKETING. CAN'T WE ALL GET ALONG? The arguments you had in 5th grade about who is more powerful, Superman or Batman, are still waged throughout the halls of B2B companies. Only now that you're all grown up it's Sales versus Marketing. Which is more important to the company? Salespeople close sales. That's the ultimate goal of both departments, but it's infinitely easier to connect sales efforts to results, than connecting marketing efforts to results. So sales wins, right?

But what if we take out the "versus"? What if Sales and Marketing collaborated? Okay, that's not a new idea, but executing on it is a bit tricky. Here are a couple of suggestions. Marketing staff— USE THE EXPERTISE OF YOUR SALESPEOPLE to understand exactly what keeps your customers up at night. Your sales staff are your boots-on-the-ground connection to the people you want to attract. Sales staff—ACT ON THE LEADS MARKETING BRINGS IN. Companies that invest in marketing often fail to reap the rewards of their efforts because no one in Sales follows up. B2B marketing exists to help prospects self-select, and to accelerate the sales cycle. Just imagine the results of combining the two superpowers you already have.

CHAPTER SIX

GET IN TOUCH WITH YOUR CUSTOMERS' FEELINGS

Sorry to break it to you but the most compelling aspect of your future marketing won't be about your brand. Or your products. It'll be about your customers.

It's a big deal when people associate your brand with a "feeling." In fact, many brands pay millions of dollars to achieve this. Why is this emotional connection so important? Because how a brand makes their customers feel is a bigger driver than product performance.

Walmart customers feel thrifty

Dove customers feel inner beauty

Campbell's customers feel comfort

Zappos customers feel happy

Nordstrom customers feel pampered

BMW customers feel elite

Disney customers feel family connection

Amazon customers feel savvy

Victoria's Secret customers feel sexy

Jeep customers feel patriotic

Apple customers feel cool

In the Mall of America, the Apple store is located right across the hall from the Microsoft store. One day after the release of a new version of iPhone and a new version of Android, industry media weighed in and gave both phones very similar scores. One had a slightly better camera and the other had a slightly longer battery life but the phones were deemed virtually equal by industry experts. But customers are not the experts.

Customers flocked to the Apple Store. These photos were taken within seconds of each other. So, if the products are virtually the same, the costs are about the same, and the release dates are exactly the same, why is the Apple store teeming with buyers while the Microsoft store is void of customers?

1 -------------------- 2 -------------------- 3 -------------------- 4 -------------------- 5

Apple has successfully connected with people on an emotional level. A level that transcends product functionality. Apple makes people feel creative, progressive and cool. Notice the special offer signs in the Microsoft store? They are taking the persuasion approach to marketing (*"Please. please, please, let us offer you a big ol' discount even before both of your feet are in our store"*) while Apple is attracting people to their brand with emotional connection and zero discounts or specials.

Why does it matter if a brand helps someone feel sexy, smart, thrifty, athletic, patriotic, etc.? I believe these emotional connections are stepping stones that lead to the biggest human drivers of all: the need to be accepted and the need to belong. Emotional connections create brand "tribes." Harley Davidson riders claim to be fiercely independent, yet the Harley Owners Group (H.O.G.) boasts over one million members. The leading H.O.G. membership benefit for these bad-ass iconoclasts? Belonging. Let's look at some examples of brand = "feeling" = tribal acceptance and belonging.

• Volvo = "I feel safe" = acceptance and belonging...as in, "I provide safety for my family and people see me as a responsible dad."

• Uponor = "I feel progressive" = acceptance and belonging...as in, "People look to me for advice and leadership."

• Under Armour = "I feel athletic" = acceptance and belonging...as in, "People consider me a serious athlete and invite me to compete."

• Canon = "I feel like a legitimate artist" = acceptance and belonging...as in, "People include me in their professional groups and forums."

• Netflix = "I feel joy" = acceptance and belonging...as in, "People think of me as a fun and culturally current member of their group."

• The Economist = "I feel intellectual" = acceptance and belonging...
as in, "I'm included in intellectual discussions and debates."

So, how do you learn what your customers want from your
brand, both rationally and emotionally? Here's a scent to follow.
• Start by talking to more of them. You can use the same survey and
steps you used for your Discovery interviews, described in chapter
three. Keep your list of marketing wishes in mind as you choose who
to chat with. For instance, if one of your wishes is to attract younger
audiences, interview lots of younger customers so you can better
understand their world view and their specific needs, desires, fears,
and other drivers behind choosing or rejecting your brand.
• Step away from the computer and go where your products or
services are being used. You will be blown away by shadowing
someone as they use your products in real-life situations. Not only
will you gain an understanding of what people like or dislike about
your product's features, you'll witness the nuances of their worlds.

You may already know the users of your industrial floor
cleaners primarily work after hours. But because of the growing
commitment to energy conservation, businesses are extinguishing
most of their lighting after 6:00 p.m. This means cleaning crews
are using your products in very low-light situations, a detail you
wouldn't know without being there. "Aha" moments may even be
grounds for changing your Brand Promise. The brand promise of
"Clean your floors FASTER" may be replaced with, "Be
CONFIDENT your floors will be super clean, even in low light
conditions." Who knows, your field trip could lead to a product
innovation like back-lit controls making your equipment more
effective and safer to use in real life conditions!

1-------------------- 2 ------------------- 3 ------------------- 4 ------------------- 5

— GUESTS KNOW BEST —

How a hotel successfully re-branded by listening.

One of the top performers of a national hotel franchise decided to go independent due to company mandates, that frankly, benefitted the brand and not their guests. The owner created the name "Legacy Hotel" and hired Dalton Brand Catalyst to guide the transformation.

Following the steps describe in this book, I interviewed about 12 past guests and a few corporate travel professionals. (People who had sent many business travelers to the hotel in recent years.) My client felt the personable staff and hot-breakfast-with-eggs-made-your-way were the top drivers of his success in the past and he planned to promote those two benefits moving forward.

Sure enough, the past guests I interviewed mentioned the friendly hotel employees and the hot break-fast. But not until *after* they told me about a more important draw of this hotel. Its location. The hotel is situated just steps from a beautiful river with hiking trails, boat tours, historic landmarks, horse-drawn carriage rides, dining, shopping, and more.

Next, I drove 4 hours to Prairie du Chien, WI to experience what I'd heard first hand. It was true. The location was charming. Pardon the pun, but the interview feedback and my visit became a wake up call for my client. He knew the town and natural attractions were a big draw, but he didn't realize the extent of just how important his location was to business and leisure travelers. In response I came back to the hotel owner with a suggestion for a different name: The River District Hotel.

Next, we created a Messaging Platform that prioritized area attractions over hotel amenities. A very bold idea for my client to embrace. There are a dozen hotels in Prairie du Chien, but the River District Hotel sits closest to the river, trails, parks, tours and landmarks, allowing them to transcend the "pancakes and room rates" battleground and carve out a unique and winable position.

The hotel's advertising and VIP box mailer (sent to travel arrangers) focused on the beautiful location.

RIVER DISTRICT
HOTEL

A PRAIRIE DU CHIEN HOTEL WITH **running water**

beautiful decor

night lights

and wake up calls

The Messaging Platform we developed for the River District Hotel was just three pages. You're well on your way creating one for your brand. It'll guide all of your marketing partners, allowing for continuity across all channels of communication. Coincidentally, today the firm that handles the hotel's email marketing program shared the results of their very first campaign. The emails got 25% click through compared to the typical 4% most marketers receive.

The architectural firm that designed the new lobby drew inspiration from the Messaging Platform and came up with this brilliant logo application. They brought living nature into the hotel lobby.

Photo courtesy of Denise Bauer

CHAPTER SEVEN

HOW TO CREATE STIMULI FOR YOUR BIGGEST, MOST IMPORTANT BRAINSTORM SESSION

Congratulations, you've made it to Week Three! Crafting the stimuli for the next, biggest, most important brainstorm session is precisely why two editors gently led me to the doors of their offices. They said this chapter of my book would leave you confused and frustrated, and that you'd probably start smoking again. I spent four decades creating advertising, so crafting the stimuli I will describe shortly comes fairly easy to me. Most of you dear readers, however, do not possess the skills to create emotion-based stimuli (stuff that looks like headlines and ads) on your own so *this* is where I strongly recommend you recruit a freelance copywriter and art director team. I will do my very best to guide you and them.

Salespeople learn how to engage prospects and close sales by trial and error. LOTS of trial and error. Marketing in all its forms, tactics and channels is crazy expensive. Too expensive to use the "trial and error" method to learn what works and what doesn't. This chapter covers how to create messaging options that clearly explain what your brand does, how it does it better, and why it matters to the world, all through the lens of your customer. Admittedly, there's no shortage of consultants, books and online programs that can help you craft your rational marketing messages. But this chapter will show you how to create, assess and agree upon emotion-driven messaging. Remember, your customers buy on emotion and validate after the fact with rational thought. Only by "trying on" a wide continuum of emotional triggers, messages, brand voices, and expressions of creative "pixie dust" can your brand find its rightful position and messaging that will catapult your brand over your competitors.

Stimuli for the BIGGEST, MOST IMPORTANT BRAINSTORM SESSION includes:

1----------------- 2 ----------------- 3 ----------------- 4 ----------------- 5

• Voice of Customer (VOC)

• Emotional Triggers

• Key Messages (Consider hiring a freelance advertising writer for this exercise.)

• Visual Articulations (Consider hiring a freelance advertising writer and art director for this exercise, too.)

HOW TO CREATE YOUR VOICE OF CUSTOMER (VOC) SOUND BITES.

"And where," you ask, "am I supposed to get the Voice of Customer sound bites?" Good question. The sound bites come right out of your Discovery interviews. Look at the answers you received from the questions.

• What are 2-3 things the company does well?

• What is the best kept secret about the company?

• What's unique about the company?

• What is the least favorite part of your job?

Many of the answers will reflect the challenges facing your customers and the solutions or advantages your company provides. Convert those problems and solutions into short VOC sound bites. Example, if the answer to the interview question, *What's unique about the ABC company?* is, *"ABC roofing materials can be walked on in extreme heat. That means I don't have to pull my crews off the job on 85+ degree days, saving me time and money."* Your sound bite captures the VOC problem or solution. Don't worry about being creative or poetic. In fact, use the language your customers use. If an answer to the question, *"What is the least favorite part of your job?"* is something like, *"I dislike the paperwork involved in every sale,"* your VOC sound bite could be, *"I wish I could avoid paperwork and just focus on selling."* Later, during the brainstorm session, your advisory committee will identify the VOC problems your brand can solve (or will solve in the future) better than your competitors, and other sound bites that will likely lead to future marketing success. Equally as important, your advisory committee will eliminate the VOC sound bites that are of lesser importance to your prospects or customers. This is the beginning of transforming your marketing from clutter to clarity and relevance.

Inside Scoop: Many of the Discovery interview responses will NOT be about your brand or its products. Rather, they will be about the industry at large, or your participants' world view or emotional state. Stuff like, "There's a shortage of workers so we can't even bid new projects." *Or* "My job is thankless." *Or,* "I'm forced to go with the cheapest supplier." *This is very valuable stuff to learn and include in your VOC sound bites. Your advisory committee may choose to shift marketing directions or add initiatives to address these needs. For instance, in response to the skilled labor shortage, your company may decide to work with technical colleges to promote skilled labor careers and advise instructors on the latest materials, tools and installation techniques. Your brand may actually ATTRACT more prospects by solving industry issues than by promoting its products and services!*

Okay, let's get to it.

• Using your Discovery interview feedback, generate as many VOC sound bites as possible.

• Then use your wisdom to weed out frivolous sound bites such as "I wish I was paid more and I had more vacation time."

• Post five or six VOC sound bites per 11x17 sheets to use in your brainstorm session. Shoot for about 4 pages totalling about 20-25

VOC sound bites for your team to discuss.

EXAMPLE OF VOICE OF CUSTOMER PAGE.

"I'd rather focus on selling, but paperwork gets in the way."

"Even a single callback can obliterate our profits."

"Sourcing roofing materials is tricky. Everyone makes similar claims so we just go with the cheapest."

"The big manufacturers don't pay attention to my needs."

"When supplies are late or damaged, production stops and we lose money."

"I wish I could get more done with fewer people."

I'll describe how to facilitate this exercise in the next chapter.

CREATING YOUR EMOTIONAL TRIGGERS.

How would you describe the people on your sales staff? Do words like, *empathetic, engaging, fun, knowledgeable, innovative, caring, cool (in a good way), passionate, confident, professional, inspiring, trustworthy* and others come to mind? Take a quick gander at your website and sales materials. Could you describe your marketing and advertising using those same words, or are they a litany of bullet points and product descriptions? Let's change that and start attracting more prospects.

Google "Emotional triggers for marketing" and you'll get dozens of suggestions. I've listed some here and checked the words I find most usable for B2B marketing purposes.

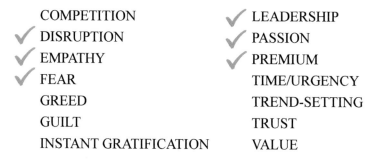

	COMPETITION	✓	LEADERSHIP
✓	DISRUPTION	✓	PASSION
✓	EMPATHY	✓	PREMIUM
✓	FEAR		TIME/URGENCY
	GREED		TREND-SETTING
	GUILT		TRUST
	INSTANT GRATIFICATION		VALUE

In my experience, discussing emotional triggers by their titles alone is too abstract for most people. But "baking" the emotional trigger into a Voice of Customer (VOC) statement gives it context and opens the door for meaningful discussion.
Create one emotional trigger sample for the most appropriate five or six words listed above. Keep in mind, I'll discuss how to facilitate this exercise in the next chapter.

Examples of Emotional Trigger stimuli:

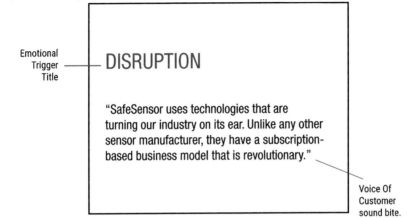

Emotional Trigger Title ——

DISRUPTION

"SafeSensor uses technologies that are turning our industry on its ear. Unlike any other sensor manufacturer, they have a subscription-based business model that is revolutionary."

Voice Of Customer sound bite.

EMPATHY

"SafeSensor takes whatever time is necessary to understand our need for accuracy and dependability. They come to our plant to make sure we successfully operate their sensors and answer any questions or concerns."

FEAR

"SafeSensor uses the strongest raw materials and most reliable components. I could buy a cheaper brand of sensor, but if it fails and causes our production line to shut down, it could cost me my job."

1-------------- 2 ------------- 3 ------------- 4 ------------- 5

LEADERSHIP

"SafeSensor never follows the pack. They lead the industry by creating new, ingenious programs and products that give us an edge on our competition."

PASSION

"The SafeSensor sales rep was so excited about how his products could help us improve and accelerate our production, I couldn't resist giving his sensors a trial run."

PREMIUM

"SafeSensor is the gold standard in the automation sensor industry. We pay more for their products but the performance and service is worth it."

Next up, creating your KEY MESSAGES.

Creating stimuli for the Key Messages segment of the upcoming brainstorm session will likely require the services of a freelance advertising copywriter. Rather than seeking this talent online, call a few local ad agencies and ask for their short list of the best freelancers in your area. While you're at it, ask about art directors, too, for the Visual Articulation segment coming up next.

Key Messages are based on the features, solutions or advantages your brand has to offer. Great products, excellent training, responsive and knowledgeable field support, a great guarantee, sustainable practices, industry-disruptive innovations, increased profitability, safety, reliability, proven outcomes, and so on. Refer to the answers your received on the Discovery interview questions:

• What are 2-3 words that describe the company?

• What are 2-3 things the company does well?

• What is the best kept secret about the company?

• What's unique about the company?

Each Key Message includes a RATIONAL STATEMENT (which you can probably write) and an EMOTIONAL STATEMENT (which your freelance talent should write).

• Start each Rational Statement with *"(Company) is successful largely because* (a)*..."* This will keep your advisory committee focused on what's *right* with your brand.

• Followed by words "largely because," then insert ONE feature, solution or advantage and colorize it. (b) That way, when you have a wall full of Key Messages, your committee participants can easily scan and select their favorite options without reading the entire statement.

• Next, using the words "SO" or "SO THAT" bridge the colorized feature, solution or advantage to a consumer benefit or outcome. (c).

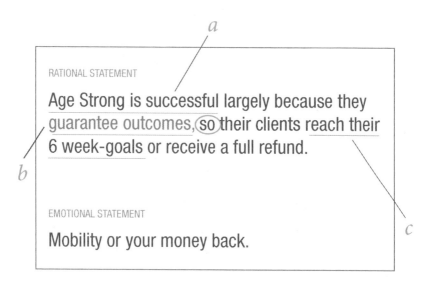

a

RATIONAL STATEMENT

Age Strong is successful largely because they guarantee outcomes, (so) their clients reach their 6 week-goals or receive a full refund.

b

EMOTIONAL STATEMENT

Mobility or your money back.

c

Inside scoop: If you can't bridge the feature or advantage to a consumer benefit or outcome, ditch that particular Key Message. Everything on your future home page, advertising or sales presentations must quickly and clearly get to what's in it for your customer.

• The EMOTIONAL STATEMENTS should be crafted by your freelance copywriter. She or he will convert the essence of your rational statement and give it some emotional and creative topspin. It'll be short and memorable, kind of like a tag line. For the purpose of your brainstorm session, she may write an original line, borrow a song title, steal a famous quote, or even grab a tag line from another company. The idea is to determine if your rational features, solutions or advantages can be stated quickly, emotionally, creatively and memorably...because PEOPLE BUY ON EMOTION.

In my practice, I generate about 20 Key Messages for use in the upcoming brainstorm session.

1---------- 2 ---------- 3 ---------- 4 ---------- 5

Age Strong is successful largely because they specialize in geriatric strength and balance training, so their clients get appropriate care, rigor and pacing.

Strength and balance for boomers and better.

Age Strong is successful largely because they customize their programs, so their clients can achieve their unique, personal goals.

Get fit with a program that fits.

Age Strong is successful largely because of their holistic approach to treatment, so their clients receive physical, nutritional, environmental and emotional care.

The complete you, improved.

1------------------ 2 ------------------ 3 ------------------ 4 ------------------ 5

Next up, VISUAL ARTICULATIONS. Creating stimuli for this portion of the brainstorm session will require the services of a freelance advertising copywriter and art director team.

Sixty-five percent of us are visual learners. According to research conducted by 3M, visuals are processed 60,000 times faster than text alone. And digital marketing is VISUAL. So it only makes sense to use visual stimuli to explore possible voices and personalities for your brand. Creating Visual Articulations is similar to creating Key Messages, only this time your freelance team will craft "ad-like" objects using words and pictures. Yup, they look a lot like ads. Your brand may never run an ad, but because we all know what an ad looks like, it's an ideal way to explore possible visual elements of your messaging.

Create one or more "ad-like objects" for each of your brand's most important features, solutions or advantages. Why more than one? You can promote a single idea using many different emotions. The examples on the next page use FEAR *(death by carpet)*, DISRUPTION *(The science will move you)* and EMPATHY *(Use a restroom* and *Two left feet)* to promote Age Strong. Same message, very different personalities. Here are some guide lines for your copywriter/art director team.

• Use good quality but inexpensive stock photos. If possible, give your art director access to your manufacturing plant and some environments where your products are in use. Have him or her take photos (with a phone...no lights, no equipment) for possible use in ad-like objects.

Inside scoop: Make sure your art director asks people if they are okay being photographed. Even if they are not posing or performing a task, some people prefer not to be photographed.

1-------------------- 2 -------------------- 3 -------------------- 4 -------------------- 5

Examples of Visual Articulation stimuli.

A carpet is seventeen
times more likely to cause
a death than a handgun.

You want yor parents to age gracefully and get the most out of life. Qerty
rolling up your beerw aqstw sder tzart sleeves and fake copy goes here.
Real, more compelling copy will be written at later date. The will happen
after learn more about what makes your bd special and valuable to your.

"Let me put it this way.
Because of my Age Strong
training, I can use a restroom
without anybody's help."

You want yor parents to age gracefully and get the most out of life. Qerty
rolling up your beerw aqstw sder tzart sleeves and fake copy goes here.
Real, more compelling copy will be written at later date. The will happen
after learn more about what makes your bd special and valuable to your.

The science behind
our Age Strong therapy
will move you.

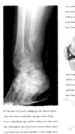

22%
GREATER MOBILITY

He'll always have
two left feet. Our job is to make
sure he stays up on them.

You want yor parents to age gracefully and get the most out of life. Qerty
rolling up your beerw aqstw sder tzart sleeves and fake copy goes here.
Real, more compelling copy will be written at later date. The will happen
after learn more about what makes your bd special and valuable to your.

1------------ 2 ------------ 3 ------------ 4 ------------ 5

• Place a logo and fake body copy at the bottom of the ad. No taglines.

• Keep the design simple so the concept is the focal point.

• Create a range of expressions from exquisite to fairly outrageous (*"Two left feet"* -to- *"Death by carpet"*) emotional triggers and personalities. Preparing a range of brand voices will help your advisory committee determine if your branding and marketing should WHISPER, TALK, or YELL in order to reflect your values and captivate your prospects.

• Open your calculator app. Let's say you developed 20 Key Messages (each depicting one specific feature, solution or advantage) for the upcoming brainstorm session. And you want to create three Visual Articulations for each of those, using various emotional triggers and personalities. Does your creative team really need to create 60 pieces of visual stimuli? Well, yes, according to your calculator...but not according to my past experience. You will need to use your judgement and select the 5 or 6 of the most important and relevant Key Messages and have your team create two ad-like objects for each (using various emotional triggers and personalities). The remaining Key Messages get one Visual Articulation. That will give your team about 25 to 27 pieces to present and lots of messages and personalities to roll around in.

Hey look! More examples of Visual Articulation stimuli.

Warning:
Not effective for
the repair of cheap
sensors or your
reputation.

Fake copy goes here. Real, more compelling copy will be written at later date. That will after learn more about what makes your brand special and valuable to your target audience copy goes here. Real.

SAFE SENSOR

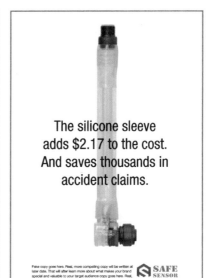

The silicone sleeve
adds $2.17 to the cost.
And saves thousands in
accident claims.

Fake copy goes here. Real, more compelling copy will be written at later date. That will after learn more about what makes your brand special and valuable to your target audience copy goes here. Real.

SAFE SENSOR

Our testing lab.

Fake copy goes here. Real, more compelling copy will be written at later date. That will after learn more about what makes your brand special and valuable to your target audience copy goes here. Real,

SAFE SENSOR

Our name says it all.

SAFE SENSOR

CHAPTER EIGHT

YOUR BIGGEST, MOST IMPORTANT BRAINSTORM SESSION

YeeHAAA. You've made it to Week Four and your BIGGEST, MOST IMPORTANT BRAINSTORM SESSION! The stimuli you will be using are:

• 6 Emotional Triggers
• Approximately 15-20 Voice Of Customer (VOC) sound bites
• Approximately 15-20 Key Messages
• Approximately 20-25 Visual Articulations
• LOTS of chocolate chip cookies

The supplies you'll need include a roll of removable painter's tape, a marker and a box of round, paper stickers (any color), about the size of a quarter, available at any office supply store. One more reminder. This 1/2 day session is immersive, fast paced and chaotic. Have fun!

BRAINSTORM SESSION TWO
PART ONE—EMOTIONAL TRIGGERS

TOTAL SESSION TIME: 4 HOURS. PART ONE: 45 MINUTES

OBJECTIVE: To select and assign the appropriate Emotional Triggers to your future marketing tactics.

DIRECTIONS:

• Start by reminding your advisory committee that emotion-based marketing stands out and commands attention. Also, remind them people buy on emotion—then validate with rational thought—so it's important to select the proper emotions that convey your brand and appropriately deliver the promises your future marketing will make.

• Next, explain that you will read the six Emotional Triggers aloud. Then, as a group, they will discuss which triggers they feel will break through *and* appropriately convey the brand.

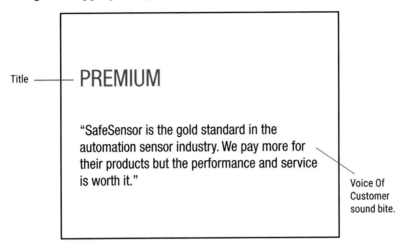

Title

PREMIUM

"SafeSensor is the gold standard in the automation sensor industry. We pay more for their products but the performance and service is worth it."

Voice Of Customer sound bite.

• Read each Emotional Trigger title followed by the Voice Of Customer sample sound bite.

• Once all the Emotional Trigger samples have been read, post them on a wall or spread them out on a table. Ask your participants which of these options feel best for your future marketing.

Inside scoop: Some groups are overwhelmed by the number of options. In those cases, ask which of these options are LEAST appropriate. Then vote those options off the island by turning them over. You'll likely get the number down to a manageable 3 or 4.

• Next, discuss each of the "survivors" and rank them. Ultimately, you'll select a Primary Emotional Trigger and a Secondary Emotional Trigger.

WAIT! I JUST LOST YOU. Let me explain. Your Primary and Secondary Emotional Triggers will be used in your future marketing communications in the "dosage" your committee prescribes. For example, a chainsaw manufacturer may decide their future messaging will primarily rely on "Premium" and use "Fear" as a Secondary Emotional Trigger. The Primary Emotional Trigger

(Premium) will guide the manufacturer's marketing team to create tactics that convey a high degree of quality, precision (and probably expensive) chainsaws and exceptional service. And along with that, their marketing creators will rely, to a lesser degree, on the Secondary Emotional Trigger (Fear) to communicate the possible consequences and dangers of buying and using inferior (and probably cheaper) chainsaws.

BRAINSTORM SESSION TWO
PART TWO—VOICE OF CUSTOMER

TIME: 45 MINUTES

OBJECTIVE: To look at your brand and its advantages through the filter of your customers, and to assess and prioritize the most critical issues your brand can solve for them.

DIRECTIONS:

• Start by reminding your advisory committee who your target prospects and customers are. Often there are multiple customer profiles such as 1) The buyers/specifiers of your products, 2) The installers of your products, 3) The end users of your products.

• Next, explain what a Voice of Customer (VOC) sound bite is (needs, fears, desires, challenges and opportunities, through the lens and language of your customers) and that you extracted them from your Discovery interviews.

• Explain that you will read the VOC sound bites one at a time and as a group, determine if the statement is VERY IMPORTANT (which means you will circle it), SOMEWHAT IMPORTANT (which means you will place a check mark near it), or NOT

IMPORTANT (which means you will draw a line through it.)

Inside Scoop: Nothing is NOT IMPORTANT. Everything your brand makes, does or says impacts the way people feel about it. But in this context, NOT IMPORTANT means a specific feature, solution or benefit is probably not important enough to dedicate future marketing dollars.

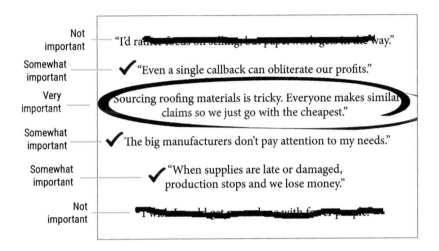

- Lastly, remind your committee that we are looking for opportunities to grow the brand and increase sales, but there are budget limitations. This exercise will help us identify and promote only the solutions our customers deem most valuable to them.
- Read aloud, discuss, and mark the level of importance to each statement. Post the pages on a wall for the duration of the session.
- Within a few days, prioritize the top circled (most important) statements based on the wisdom of the group and your own opinion. Then prioritize the statements that are checked (somewhat important). Send the list to your advisory committee members. Include your commentary stating future marketing will be based on this hierarchy of messages/customer needs.

1-------------- 2 -------------- 3 -------------- 4 -------------- 5

BRAINSTORM SESSION TWO
PART THREE—KEY MESSAGES

TIME: 60 MINUTES

OBJECTIVE: To determine and prioritize the Key Messages that differentiate your brand and are most compelling and valuable to your customers.

DIRECTIONS:

• Have your 15-20 Key Messages, marker, round stickers and blue painter's tape ready for action.

• Ask for a volunteer to help you tape Key Messages to a wall after you read each one aloud to the group.

• Start by explaining the Discovery interviews revealed or confirmed your brand has a lot to offer. Things like great products, excellent training, knowledgeable field support, a great guarantee, sustainable practices, industry-disruptive innovations, improved safety, reliability, proven outcomes, and so on. The problem is, your prospects can't possibly retain all these things, so today the group will have to winnow the selections down to the most compelling and valuable features, solutions and advantages your brand delivers. Remind them each Key Message will reflect only ONE benefit per message.

• Explain each Key Message will include a RATIONAL articulation of a solution, feature or advantage, and an EMOTIONAL articulation, which will be short and memorable, much like a tag line. We do this to determine if our rational solutions can be stated in short sound bites. Digital channels and the expectations of today's busy prospects require messaging to be short, valuable and memorable.

• Ask the group to allow you to read all of the Key Messages and withhold their comments until you have finished. Ask your volunteer to tape each one to the wall after you read it.

• Once the Key Messages have been read and you've turned your conference room wall into a fire hazard of paper, have each participant (including yourself) take six stickers and place one on each of their favorite six Key Messages. They can "vote" for any messages for any reason, such as their fondness of a particular rational offering, or the personality of an emotional statement. Set a time limit of 10 minutes for placing their stickers. Let them discuss the options among themselves if they wish. When all of the stickers have been placed, ask everyone to sit down for group discussion.

• For the next several minutes you'll be bouncing around like an over -caffeinated game show host. Quickly review and discuss each Key Message beginning with those with the most stickers, and work your way down to the Key Messages that have only one. Ask those who placed a sticker on the Key Message you are discussing to explain why they gravitated to that message. Make notes right on the Key Messages so you don't lose comments or suggestions.

• When you've covered every message that received votes, ask your group if there are any Key Messages they DISLIKED, and why. Understanding what participants disliked will help you and your marketing team avoid these messages in future marketing — OR— give you or others in the group an opportunity to defend that particular message.

Inside scoop: Challenging a person who disliked a Key Message may be a difficult or sensitive discussion. But it is far more timely, prudent and effective to haggle over relatively inexpensive Key Messages in the safety of a conference room, than to have the same discussion after hundreds, if not thousands of dollars have been spent developing a website or advertising based on that message. Most of the time, you'll reach a consensus. Occasionally, an advisory committee must agree to disagree in order to keep the brainstorm session moving.

• Leave the Key Messages on the wall.

BRAINSTORM SESSION TWO
PART FOUR— VISUAL ARTICULATIONS

60 MINUTES

OBJECTIVE: To determine and prioritize the Visual Articulations that differentiate your brand and are most captivating to your customers.

DIRECTIONS: You and your advisory committee will discuss and prioritize several Visual Articulations. This is similar to the Key Messages exercise.

• Have your 15-20 Visual Articulations, a marker, round stickers and blue painter's tape ready for action.

• Ask for a volunteer to help you tape Visual Articulations to a wall after you read each aloud to the group.

• Remind them the Discovery interviews revealed or confirmed our brand has a lot to offer—stuff we saw in the Key Messages exercise. Each Visual Articulation will reflect ONE benefit or advantage.

• Next, explain that, while we are not recommending ads at this time, we all know what an ad looks like. So we will use "ad-like" objects to convey various messages using visual elements. And visuals greatly influence how a message is interpreted and processed.

• Ask the group to allow you to read each Visual Articulation and hold their comments until you have finished. Have your volunteer tape each Visual Articulation to the wall after you've read it.

• Once all the Visual Articulations are read and posted on the wall, have each participant (including yourself) take six stickers and place

one on each of their favorite six Visual Articulations. They can "vote" for any message for any reason. Set a time limit of 10 minutes. Let them discuss the options among themselves if they wish. When all of the stickers have been placed, ask everyone to sit down for discussion.

• Review and discuss each Visual Articulation beginning with the ones that received the most stickers, working your way down to those with only one sticker. High vote messages will play a prominent role in your future marketing and sales presentations. Ask those who placed a sticker on the Visual Articulation you are discussing to explain why they gravitated to that selection. Make notes directly on the papers so you don't lose comments.

• When you've covered every message that received votes, ask your group if there are any Visual Articulations they DISLIKED, and why. Similar to the Key Message exercise, this will help you and your marketing team avoid certain messages in future marketing—OR—give you or others in the group an appropriate time and place to defend that particular articulation.

• Thank the committee for their time and input!

• Help yourself to the last chocolate chip cookie.

ROB POV

DON'T WIMP OUT.

Asking for feedback on your brand's Key Messages and
Visual Articulations doesn't mean you have to accept every
point made. In fact, you shouldn't. Feedback may be
conflicting. Some may not "tee up" compelling marketing
or reflect the values of your brand. Before you begin your
brainstorm session, post this marketing recipe for success,
"STAND OUT - BE VALUABLE - TELL THE TRUTH."
As feedback is discussed, refer to the recipe to
defend your guidance toward messages that make an
emotional connection with future customers. This is the
stuff that pushes the outer limits of the captivation
continuum; exquisite on one end, outrageous on the other.
Because you know the messaging in the middle is boring
and won't even get noticed.

So, before your brainstorm session begins, ask for
the group's permission to stir up the pot. To challenge your
current marketing. And to explore ideas that will make their
palms sweat a little. Remind them the discussion is about
creating a Messaging Platform only. None of the stimuli is
intended to be seen "as is" to the outside world. This
allows for open and productive discussion.

WHY DID WE DO THIS STUFF AND WHAT'S NEXT? That's the question you'll be asked before your advisory committee adjourns. According to the schedule, you have 30 minutes remaining to answer this question but you can get in done in 10. Here's how:

• Explain that input gathered in the brainstorm session today will help you build a Messaging Platform. This foundational document will be used by internal and external marketing partners as they create tactics for your brand. From now on your marketing will be consistently on-brand, compelling, and deliver real value to prospective customers. The Messaging Platform will look like this.

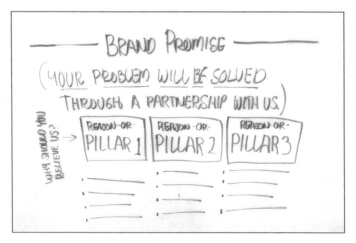

    - We will base our marketing on a bold BRAND PROMISE. This promise will be a solution our brand is uniquely qualified to provide. A solution our customers crave.

    - We will assume every prospect who sees this promise will say (or at least think) "Why should I believe this promise?" Our answer comes in the form of three SUPPORT PILLARS that, when combined, provides proof and differentiates our brand.

    - Under the SUPPORT PILLARS are granular talking points.

CHAPTER NINE

CREATING A MESSAGING PLATFORM THAT SETS YOUR BRAND APART

Welcome to Week Five and the creation of your Messaging Platform!

Most Messaging Platforms are 30-60 pages long. The reason for such excess? To justify the $60,00-$80,000 most branding consultants charge. Yours will be just three pages. The three pages that matter. Your Messaging Platform will be on brand and easy for internal and external marketing partners to understand. And it will include leadership-approved foundational elements gleaned from the Biggest, Most Important Brainstorm Session.

Page one of your Messaging Platform will serve as your Value Proposition, an inward-focused declaration of your brand. Soon, everyone in your organization will understand and rally around the value your brand provides.

WHAT WE DO	*Not fancy. Not schmancy. Just clear and concise.*
HOW WE DO IT BETTER	*The features and solutions that differentiate your brand from the others.*
WHY/HOW WE MATTER TO OTHERS	*Why and how you want your brand to positively affect individuals, industries, communities, the world.*
WHY NOW	*Want to win business? Relevance is everything.*

Let's create a Value Proposition for your brand. Refer to the brainstorm session results and follow these steps. As you saw on the previous page, I do not advocate crafting a one or two sentence Value Proposition. Too much is sacrificed for the sake of brevity.

• Select one or two smart and trusted members of your advisory committee to collaborate with you.

• Craft your short and concise WHAT WE DO statement. Example: We make sensors that detect foreign particles during food production. —or—We make storm gutters for residential homes. —or—We manufacture advanced ditch digging equipment. Remember, your WHAT WE DO statement should be jargon-free and easily understandable to your next door neighbor. It should *not* sound anything like, "We are a solutions based provider of next generation water dispersion blah, blah, blah. Just for fun, compare your new WHAT WE DO statement with the wording you currently use on your website's home page or sales materials. Better? Clearer? Good.

• Craft your HOW WE DO IT BETTER statement. This statement reveals what makes your brand amazing, unique and preferred. It is the people, processes, products, features, solutions and advantages that, when combined, captivate prospects and make your brand. Your brainstorm session results point to the many ways your company does it better. The wisdom of your advisory committee directed you to the top 3 or 4. Example:

    - Our peerless commitment to contamination-free food

    - Our proprietary technologies detect foreign matter 28% smaller than the leading brand's sensors.

    - Our dedicated Quick Response Team will repair or replace damaged sensors within 4 hours, guaranteed.

• Craft your WHY AND HOW WE MATTER TO OTHERS statement. Your brand exists for a reason. When individuals engage with your brand their lives are improved, new tribes are created, industries are disrupted (in a good way), and just maybe, the world becomes a better place. Here are some WHY AND HOW WE MATTER TO OTHERS examples;

- INDIVIDUALS' lives are improved because our mobile urgent care clinics come to patients, resulting in convenience, quicker diagnoses and faster recoveries.

- HOSPITALS are more profitable because without our services many peoples' only choice for medical treatment is the emergency room. A significant subset of this population is unable to pay, leaving the hospital to absorb the $3000 + costs.

- COMMUNITIES with limited or no brick and mortar medical facilities are able to promise quality, local care, thus raising the appeal and livability of the area.

- THE NATION gets a break on health insurance costs because overall treatment costs go down.

Next, I want to share some thoughts on your WHY NOW statement. Communicating the right message to the right people is imperative to your marketing success. Communicating the right message to the right people at the *right time* will improve your hit rate even more. WHY NOW includes two important aspects of timing: Trigger Events and Converging Forces.

Trigger Events are those things that suddenly appear on your radar screen that can negatively or positively affect your business. They are typically beyond your control (like the wind) but require thoughtful, nimble action (like adjusting your sails) from your marketing department. Let's say your company manufactures power ditch trenching equipment. Here are a few Trigger Event examples:

- An unexpected, new mandate to bury gas, cable and power lines in several major suburbs goes into effect, creating a temporary surge in demand for digging equipment.

- A machine component from another country suddenly becomes unavailable, adversely affecting production.

-Your biggest customer lands a huge contract and is counting on you and your equipment to help them meet extreme demands.

I don't market my services on a perpetual basis. That costs too much. Instead, I wait in the weeds until certain Trigger Events make my prospects likely to need my services. Trigger Events I follow include changes in company CMOs, Mergers and Acquisitions and announcements of expansions and new product categories. All of these Trigger Events are easily found on LinkedIn and through the use of inexpensive business intel search engines. My favorite intel engine is www.sellingintel.com. In the interest of transparency, this tool was developed by Sam Richter, a client and personal friend.

Converging Forces are broad-based, tectonic shifts in industries, the economy, technology, social/cultural/political trends and so on. In 1867, the invention of refrigerated railroad cars allowed long distance shipment of fresh dairy, produce, beer and meat. For the first time, people far from the source could buy and enjoy these perishable products. Because of a technological advancement in refrigeration, the dairy, produce, beer and meat industries experienced a growth explosion.

Oddly, a Converging Force of technology was mentioned in the Broadway hit, Jersey Boys.

In the early 1950s, the second consumer product to use a breakthrough technology called transistors was (you guessed it) the transistor radio. Around the same time these space age circuits became an affordable radio component, a cultural shift was taking place. Young people were developing an appetite for a new music genre called rock 'n' roll. As discussed in the show, tiny transistor radios became the music delivery device-of-choice for teenagers. Now they could rock out to Elvis and Jerry Lee, right under the noses of their over-protective-yet-oblivious parents. This convergence led to explosive growth in transistor radio sales. And rock 'n' roll bands.

As not discussed in the show, the *first* consumer product to use transistor technology was the hearing aid. Hmmm, could it be they had an evil (and very long tail) strategy to get tender young ears hooked on rock 'n' roll so they could sell them radios in their teens and hearing aids in their 70s?

Converging Forces are great sales pitch openers. Before I get to that, here's how NOT to open a sales meeting. "We're not just a widget manufacturer. We're problem solvers." (Followed by a list of problems your brand solves.) Well, that's a problem. Because this approach can be off-putting and formulaic. Meaning, you'll sound pretty much like every brand in your industry. Typical sales presentations (and websites) open with a laundry list of problems they solve like:

• "Other" trench diggers require a new blade every 3 months and that means big expense and down time.

• "Other" trench diggers can't tell a gas line from a tree root, so crews are in constant danger.

• "Other" trench equipment companies treat their customers like a number.

It's a crap shoot because these are problems your prospect may or may not actually have. So rather than start your presentation with problems, a more captivating opener is an observation about a Converging Force your prospect should know about. A Converging Force that could become an OPPORTUNITY for your prospect, if they partner with your brand. Here are a few examples:

- The infrastructure industry is converting to robotic equipment. Those who have done so are reaping big rewards.

- The average skilled worker in the United States is 57 years old and there is very little talent in the pipeline. Collaborative manufacturer/industry leader/technical college training programs are a bright spot in the labor shortage epidemic.

- Innovative municipalities have figured out how to stretch their budgets by joint ownership of heavy equipment with neighboring communities.

Starting your sales pitch with Converging Forces and related opportunities tees up your prospect for deeper engagement with your brand.

Okay, let's craft your WHY NOW statement.

• Identify 3-4 Trigger Events and 3-4 Converging Forces you feel are especially relevant to prospects who wish to avoid the pitfalls or leverage the opportunities that come with change.

Inside scoop: Consult with colleagues and industry experts to gather information. Sales, field support and other customer-facing professionals in your organization may be able to share Trigger Events. Leadership and industry experts are likely to be aware of Converging Forces.

• Craft your WHY NOW statement based on a combo platter of the three most compelling Trigger Events and/or Converging Forces your prospect should know about. Clearly state the situation and how partnering with your brand will help your prospects thrive and/or avoid failure. At this point you have all the ingredients to craft the Value Proposition page of your Messaging Platform. It takes a ton of effort to get this far, but you can do it. Every word will be understandable, relevant and important. Here's an example of page one:

WHAT WE DO	XYZ TrenchCo manufactures trench diggers for utility, industrial and commercial applications.
HOW WE DO IT BETTER	SAFER— Our GPS and sonar detection technology prevent accidental power/gas line, water line and cable cutting. INNOVATIVE TRAINING— Our training program is attracting new talent to the industry. COST SAVINGS— Robotics allow for fewer workers and 30%-50% faster trenching.
WHY/HOW WE MATTER TO OTHERS	Operators are safer because they use robotic controls several feet from the cutting blades. Our training program is attracting new talent and generating high paying jobs. Municipalities and commercial owners stay on schedule and save money. Communities experience shorter traffic interruptions and fewer detours during trenching.
WHY NOW	We have viable solutions to our nation's skilled labor shortage and aging infrastructure. Job site safety concerns and liability exposure can be cut in half. Profit margin trajectories have been flat or downward for over decade. Until now.

Page two of your Messaging Platform is your Messaging Ladder, a consumer-facing version of your Value Proposition. Simply put, the Messaging Ladder is a hierarchy of your messaging relative to the needs of your customers. This template is included in the Toolkit.

Here's a Messaging Ladder template with descriptions.

| BRAND PROMISE | *The broad based solution you provide to your prospects' problems. It's similar to a value proposition, but stated through the lens of your customer.* |

The combined three Support Pillars make your brand special and unique.

SUPPORT PILLAR 1	SUPPORT PILLAR 2	SUPPORT PILLAR 3
A compelling reason your brand is uniquely able to live up to your Brand Promise.	*A compelling reason your brand is uniquely able to live up to your Brand Promise.*	*A compelling reason your brand is uniquely able to live up to your Brand Promise.*
PILLAR 1 TALKING POINTS	**PILLAR 2 TALKING POINTS**	**PILLAR 3 TALKING POINTS**
• *Granular talking points that back up this Pillar.* • *Granular talking points that back up this Pillar.* • *Granular talking points that back up this Pillar.*	• *Granular talking points that back up this Pillar.* • *Granular talking points that back up this Pillar.* • *Granular talking points that back up this Pillar.*	• *Granular talking points that back up this Pillar.* • *Granular talking points that back up this Pillar.* • *Granular talking points that back up this Pillar.*

| EMOTIONAL TRIGGERS | *Primary and secondary triggers.* |

| VALUES | *List of up to five Brand Values (behaviors).* |

| PREFERENCES | *List of DOs and DON'Ts regarding how the brand is to be articulated through language and imagery. Preferences may have come up in brainstorm session 2.* |

| HERO STATEMENT | *The hero of your Brand Story is not your brand. It's your customer. This statement reflects how you want your customers to FEEL because they engaged with your brand.* |

Here's an example of a finished Messaging Ladder.

| BRAND PROMISE | XYZ TrenchCo Innovations allow you to meet the demands of a changing world while significantly increasing your profits and improving worker safety. |

| 1) INNOVATIVE TECHNOLOGY | 2) INNOVATIVE MATERIALS | 3) INNOVATIVE TRAINING & SUPPORT |

| TALKING POINTS | TALKING POINTS | TALKING POINTS |

- Our equipment requires fewer workers to operate
- Experience 30%-50% faster trenching
- Increased safety—our proprietary detection technology helps operators avoid existing lines.
- Robotics allow operators to work several feet away from moving parts

- Our equipment is built to last 15 years (5 years longer than the leading brand)
- Our cutting blades last 3x longer, resulting in less downtime
- Controls are protected by heavy duty shields

- On-boarding includes an Emergency Action Plan so unexpected events can be dealt with quickly
- Our innovative training program is attracting new talent and placing them in 6 months
- Our phones are answered by real people within 3 rings
- 1-day field support guarantee

| EMOTIONAL TRIGGERS | Primary: Innovation — Secondary: Premium |

| VALUES | Responsive, Safety First, Innovation-driven |

| PREFERENCES |

DO connect product features and benefits with provable outcomes
DO include a call-to-action when possible
DO tie innovation with increased ease, and/ or safety and/or profits

DON'T use industry jargon
DON'T disparage our competitors
DON'T use blue (competitor's color)
DON'T focus on price or discounts

| HERO STATEMENT | "I feel PROGRESSIVE because I chose a partner that delivers new technologies, giving my company better ways to meet growing demands, earn higher profits and keep workers safe." |

1------------ 2 ------------ 3 ------------ 4 ------------ 5

Page three is a Narrative Story based on the Messaging Ladder. By now you may be muttering to yourself, "Hey Rob, this is starting to feel redundant." Here's the deal. Some of your internal and external marketing partners will get what they need from your Value Proposition on page one. Others will want to understand the hierarchy of your messaging, and the Messaging Ladder on page two provides that. Still others will interpret your brand story better in narrative form. That's page three. Heres a template of the Narrative Story with descriptions.

| **OUR STORY** | *An 80 to 100 word narrative that includes where you conduct business, what problems you solve for your customers, how your brand is uniquely qualified to solve those problems, why your solutions are needed now. And lastly, how your customers feel because they do business with your brand.* |

| **THE SHORT STORY** | *Sometimes referred to as an "elevator speech," this three to four sentence explanation of your brand gives an overview and leaves your prospect wanting more.* |

| **THE FLIP SIDE** | *A reverse-view of why you exist. Rather than start with your brand and your solutions, it is a rejection of the status quo or flawed industry "norms."* |

An example of the finished Narrative Story on page three.

OUR STORY

XYZ TrenchCo is an independently owned, Dallas-based, manufacturer of high-tech trench diggers for utility, industrial and commercial infrastructure applications. We innovate and provide proprietary robotic digging equipment that significantly reduces job site accidents while increasing productivity and profitability. Our equipment runs longer between required maintenance so there's less downtime. Our nation's workforce is shrinking, our underground power, water, sewer, and gas systems are aging, and the demand for next generation cable service is at an all-time high. Our customers actively seek innovative ways to meet the demands of today's customers. XYZ TrenchCo helps them meet these needs at the highest level of training, safety, speed and profitability. The result; our buyers feel progressive for issuing equipment that keeps crews productive and safe, and for helping their companies net higher profits.

THE SHORT STORY

Our nation's labor shortage, aging infrastructure and high demand for next generation cable service has put an unprecedented strain on trench and installation companies. XYZ TrenchCo makes innovative trench digging equipment that meets these challenges at the highest level of training, safety, speed and profitability.

At XYZ TrenchCo, we reject the idea that increased demand automatically means adding personnel and working longer hours. Rather than breaking your back and the bank, consider breaking away from conventional digging equipment. XYZ TrenchCo's innovative equipment and solutions help you meet customer needs at the highest level of safety, speed and profitability.

STOP. You have what you need to hunker down and create your Messaging Platform.

Good luck. I'll miss you while we're apart.

You did it! YOU HAVE COMPLETED YOUR MESSAGING PLATFORM. By involving your stakeholders, allowing them to roll up their sleeves, weigh the options, share their opinions, express their knowledge and passion, AND REACH A CONSENSUS, you are locked and loaded to power up your B2B branding and create more effective marketing tactics faster and for less money than ever. (No wonder your competitors will hate you.) Feel free to design your Messaging Platform within your own corporate graphic standards. Here's an example.

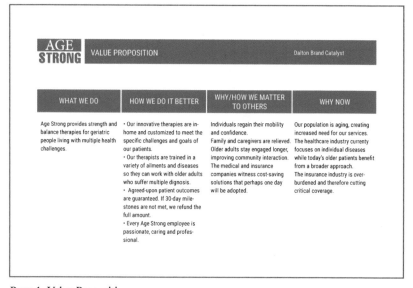

Page 1 Value Proposition

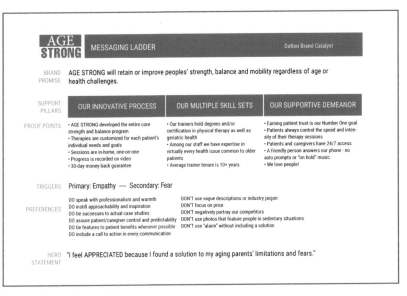

AGE STRONG — MESSAGING LADDER — Dalton Brand Catalyst

BRAND PROMISE: AGE STRONG will retain or improve peoples' strength, balance and mobility regardless of age or health challenges.

SUPPORT PILLARS:

OUR INNOVATIVE PROCESS	OUR MULTIPLE SKILL SETS	OUR SUPPORTIVE DEMEANOR
PROOF POINTS: • AGE STRONG developed the entire core strength and balance program • Therapies are customized for each patient's individual needs and goals • Sessions are in-home, one-on-one • Progress is recorded on video • 30-day money-back guarantee	• Our trainers hold degrees and/or certification in physical therapy as well as geriatric health • Among our staff we have expertise in virtually every health issue common to older patients • Average trainer tenure is 10+ years	• Earning patient trust is our Number One goal • Patients always control the speed and intensity of their therapy sessions • Patients and caregivers have 24/7 access • A friendly person answers our phone - no auto prompts or "on hold" music • We love people!

TRIGGERS: Primary: Empathy — Secondary: Fear

PREFERENCES:
DO speak with professionalism and warmth
DO instill approachability and inspiration
DO tie successes to actual case studies
DO assure patient/caregiver control and predictability
DO tie features to patient benefits whenever possible
DO include a call to action in every communication

DON'T use vague descriptions or industry jargon
DON'T focus on price
DON'T negatively portray our competitors
DON'T use photos that feature people in sedentary situations
DON'T use "alarm" without including a solution

HERO STATEMENT: "I feel APPRECIATED because I found a solution to my aging parents' limitations and fears."

Page 2 Messaging Ladder

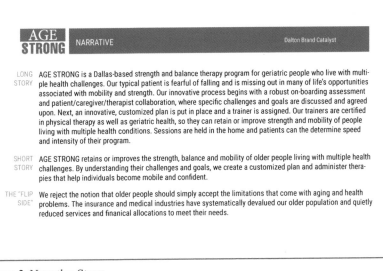

AGE STRONG — NARRATIVE — Dalton Brand Catalyst

LONG STORY: AGE STRONG is a Dallas-based strength and balance therapy program for geriatric people who live with multiple health challenges. Our typical patient is fearful of falling and is missing out in many of life's opportunities associated with mobility and strength. Our innovative process begins with a robust on-boarding assessment and patient/caregiver/therapist collaboration, where specific challenges and goals are discussed and agreed upon. Next, an innovative, customized plan is put in place and a trainer is assigned. Our trainers are certified in physical therapy as well as geriatric health, so they can retain or improve strength and mobility of people living with multiple health conditions. Sessions are held in the home and patients can the determine speed and intensity of their program.

SHORT STORY: AGE STRONG retains or improves the strength, balance and mobility of older people living with multiple health challenges. By understanding their challenges and goals, we create a customized plan and administer therapies that help individuals become mobile and confident.

THE "FLIP SIDE": We reject the notion that older people should simply accept the limitations that come with aging and health problems. The insurance and medical industries have systematically devalued our older population and quietly reduced services and finanical allocations to meet their needs.

Page 3 Narrative Story

Inside scoop: I've talked a lot about creating an emotional bond with your customers and how your brand may ultimately help them find a new tribe or gain greater acceptance within their current tribes. I know this can sound kind of abstract so let's take a minute to look at how the Hero Statement, "I feel PROGRESSIVE" can lead to acceptance and belonging.

> "I Feel PROGRESSIVE for partnering with a company that delivers innovative technologies that allow my company to meet growing demands, earn higher profits and keep workers safe."

> MY CREW APPRECIATES ME because I invested in equipment that helps them get more done in less time, safer. LEADERSHIP APPRECIATES ME because our company nets higher profits. INDUSTRY EXPERTS RESPECT ME because I'm trying cutting edge technologies that are sure to disrupt the industry.

> I feel ACCEPTED and I BELONG to these tribes.

Armed with a Messaging Platform, your marketing tactics will get traction like never before. But there's still one more critical step before your team begins to build out marketing tactics. A Creative Brief. Learn more in Chapter Ten.

CHAPTER TEN

FINALLY, BRANDED MESSAGING THAT DRIVES SALES AND GROWS YOUR BUSINESS

Your Messaging Platform is applied to ALL communications and its purpose is to build long term brand equity and trust between the company and your customers. Your Creative Brief is a road map that guides your creative team as they prepare tactics to promote specific products or services. The Creative Brief plainly explains the advantage along with other critical information. Creating a marketing tactic without a Creative Brief sets up your marketing department, and the tactic itself, for failure. Let's walk through each point and I'll provide sample answers to each question.

• DATE: (You got this one, Sport.)

• PREPARED BY: The individual requesting a tactic is responsible to provide this information. Offer assistance if necessary.

• PROJECT TITLE: Yup, give each project a title so you can easily find and update it when necessary. Example: RoboDig product introduction 2019 trade show graphics.

• JOB NUMBER: Assign a job number. If you have not created a numbering system, do so now. It can be simple. I suggest you use a 2+4 digit system. The first 2 digits indicate the year the tactic was created followed by four numbers beginning with 0001. Example for the first project of 2019: JOB NUMBER: 19-0001.

DALTON BRAND CATALYST | CREATIVE BRIEF

Date:
Prepared by:
Project Title:
Job Number: Approval_____

DESCRIBE THE COMMUNICATION TACTIC YOU NEED. (BROCHURE, SALES PRESENTATION, AD CAMPAIGN, ETC.)

WHO ARE THE INTENDED AUDIENCE(S)? (PRIMARY, SECONDARY)

WHAT ARE THE PROBLEMATIC INSIGHTS OR PERCEPTIONS THAT MATTER TO THIS AUDIENCE(S) OR SITUATION?

WHAT IS THE SINGULAR SOLUTION YOU WISH TO CONVEY?

WHY SHOULD OUR AUDIENCE(S) BELIEVE THIS?

WHAT IS THE DESIRED OUTCOME/GOAL?

HOW WILL THE EFFECTIVENESS/SUCCESS OF THIS PROJECT BE MEASURED?

WHAT ARE THE SPECIAL CHALLENGES?

WHAT IS THE BUDGET TO ACCOMPLISH THIS REQUEST?

WHAT IS THE DEADLINE FOR THIS PROJECT?

ARE THERE ANY MANDATES OR LEGAL REQUIREMENTS WE NEED TO BE AWARE OF?

A Creative Brief template is included in the Toolkit available at www.daltonbrandcatalyst.com.

• APPROVAL: This is the most important entry on your Creative Brief. If you are the person responsible for approving and funding the creation of a tactic, great. But if that responsibility belongs to anyone else in your organization, you MUST get it signed BEFORE your team begins to build out any tactic, for three very important reasons.

Reason One: You'll need definitive, agreed-upon information in order to hit the messaging "bulls eye" and create a relevant tactic.

Reason Two: If, for whatever reason, you don't understand the information or don't agree with it, it's far better to get clarity or register your concerns *before* you build out the tactic.

Reason Three: I don't want you to be blind-sided by someone (head of sales, your CEO) who "just can't remember" giving you certain information *after* your team has spent hours and hours on the creation of the tactic.

Inside scoop: You will get push back on this. But training your colleagues and leadership to provide details and grant approval BEFORE commencing on a project will pay huge dividends and earn you some respect along the way.

Okay, now on to the questions in your Creative Brief.

DESCRIBE THE COMMUNICATION TACTIC YOU NEED.
This question requires the person making the request to be specific and not allow for "scope creep" (adding more tactics to the project). Example: Trade show booth graphics for two 4 ft. by 10 ft. panels. (If they realize they need a trade show brochure, too, they must formally add that to the tactics list so you can accurately plan and price the project.)

WHO ARE THE INTENDED AUDIENCE(S)? (PRIMARY, SECONDARY)

Example: Primary— Equipment procurement officers at the largest 500 construction companies that specialize in infrastructure applications.

Secondary— City and Municipal Planners/Managers.

Not all projects will have multiple target audiences.

WHAT ARE THE PROBLEMATIC INSIGHTS OR PERCEPTIONS THAT MATTER TO THIS AUDIENCE(S) OR SITUATION?

In other words, what keeps them up at night? Consider writing this in the voice of your audience. Example: "Our infrastructure is aging and repairs are mounting. I don't have the budget to buy lots of equipment. I need a trench digger that can do more in less time."

WHAT IS THE SINGULAR SOLUTION YOU WISH TO CONVEY?

The trick is keeping it SINGULAR. Remember, great B2B marketing won't close the sale. But it will attract and hold their attention so you get the opportunity to tell them more at the trade show, or on your website. Example: We want to introduce RoboDig innovative machinery that digs 30%-50% faster than any other digger in the industry.

WHY SHOULD OUR AUDIENCES BELIEVE THIS?

Your PILLARS and talking points will likely cover this but there may also be some new data or proof points that back your claim. Example: Our new demo video will debut at the trade show in August. It proves the digger's speed and power.

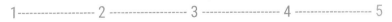

WHAT IS THE DESIRED OUTCOME?

The answer is best if it's measurable. Example: 400 completed demo request forms from prospective customers that visit our trade show booth in August.

HOW WILL THE EFFECTIVENESS/SUCCESS OF THIS PROJECT BE MEASURED?

Different tactics require different means and metrics for measuring effectiveness. Online advertising and social media is trackable using Google Analytics and countless other measurement technologies. Print and broadcast media can only give you a general (and biased) number of eyeballs that see your message (most belonging to people who don't need or want what you are selling). For measuring the effectiveness of retail and e-commerce promotions, the best metric is sales. Example for this Creative Brief: Number of completed request-for-demo forms.

WHAT ARE THE SPECIAL CHALLENGES?

This information is to help the creators understand the context or circumstances that could impact this particular message or tactic. Example: This year our trade show booth is located near the back of the DCA Convention Center so our key graphics and logo must be placed at the top third of the booth so convention attendees can see it from the entry doors.

WHAT IS THE BUDGET TO ACCOMPLISH THIS REQUEST?

If you have never asked this question before, you need to start now. It's okay if the question is turned back to you in the form of a request for an estimate, but reach an agreement on budget, *before* you begin creating. Example: Booth Graphics $15,000. Must include photography fees and printing.

WHAT IS THE DEADLINE FOR THIS PROJECT?

It's up to you to build in check points along the way. Deadlines for internal approval must allow time to make adjustments and prepare final files for the publication or production deadline. Example: First check-in with Bill Smith, 10/17. Final approval 10/25. Send files to publication 11/7.

ARE THERE ANY MANDATES OR LEGAL REQUIREMENTS WE NEED TO BE AWARE OF?

This question is intended to inform creators of legal and mandated stuff. Example: Regarding the request to place key graphics near the top of our booth, be advised DCA Convention Center does not allow graphics, banners or balloons to extend above ten feet from the floor.

By using your Messaging Platform and your Creative Brief, you and your marketing team will work smarter and create tactics that work harder and drive business.

ROB POV

USE AS FEW WORDS POSSIBLE TO MAKE YOUR POINT.

We are at the typical conclusion of my Branding and Messaging Platform gigs. Thank you for reading my book and embarking on this journey. Beginning right now your branding and marketing efforts will be more captivating, more valuable and more relevant. They'll be completed faster. They'll be on brand. They'll make emotional connections with your prospects. They'll be super efficient and perform in today's digital marketplace. They'll drive business. Approval processes will become much easier and accelerated. And there will be far fewer "do-overs."

Beginning today, your culture will start to shift. Employees will feel a higher level of pride in your brand, what your company provides to the world, and the role they play to make lives better.

Get out there and power up your B2B branding. And make your competitors hate you.

BUT WAIT! THERE'S MORE!

As an extra bonus I'm throwing in WEEK 6 absolutely FREE!

(What can I say. I'm a giver.)

CHAPTER ELEVEN

MOVING YOUR MESSAGING PLATFORM FROM PAPER TO PEOPLE

We've discussed the benefits of your Messaging Platform relative to improving your branded messaging such as websites, sales pitches and advertising. But the first step in putting your new Messaging Platform to work actually starts with your internal audience—the owners and management team, sales staff, employees and other stakeholders. Simply making them aware of your new Messaging Platform won't necessarily lead to better marketing. But involving them in the integration of your new Messaging Platform, relative to their role in the company, results in a better understanding of the brand, heightened pride and advocacy, and improved customer experiences.

Inside scoop: The behavior and attitude of your staff matter more to your customers than your branding and advertising ever will. That's why it's critical to involve them in the integration of your new Messaging Platform.

BRAINSTORM SESSION THREE
MESSAGING PLATFORM INTEGRATION

TIME: 2 HOURS.

OBJECTIVE: To help employees and key stakeholders understand, "own" and promote the new Messaging Platform.

DIRECTIONS: This session will require one large room and if possible, a few breakout rooms. If extra rooms are not available, you can assign cohorts to the corners of the large room.

• Invite up to 25 participants including leaders and worker bees.

• At the beginning of this session, explain that over the past 35 days a marketing advisory committee has been reimagining the branding and our messaging in order to significantly grow market share and increase profitability.

• Post the new Brand Promise, the three Support Pillars and the Hero Statement on the wall. Explain that the Brand Promise is a bold declaration of a big problem your brand solves. The Support Pillars are the top three reasons your company can live up to the Brand Promise, and when combined, differentiates the brand from all others. Next, point to the Hero Statement. Explain this is how you want your customers to feel because they chose to engage with, and buy from your brand. (Example: "I feel PROGRESSIVE because I partner with a company that brings new and intelligent technologies and solutions to meet growing demands). In other words, the Hero Statement is the "happily ever after" part of our future powerful and focused marketing.

BRAND PROMISE

XYZ TrenchCo innovation allows you to meet the unprecedented demands of a changing world while significantly increasing your profits and worker safety.

SUPPORT PILLAR 1 **INNOVATIVE TECHNOLOGY**	SUPPORT PILLAR 2 **INNOVATIVE MATERIALS**	SUPPORT PILLAR 3 **INNOVATIVE SUPPORT**

HERO STATEMENT

"I feel PROGRESSIVE because I partner with a company that brings new and intelligent technologies and solutions to meet growing demands."

• Give your group an opportunity to ask questions, but assure them that everything they see is subject to fine-tuning before it goes live for to the world to see.

• Ask the group to call out "above the ground" marketing channels and tactics. (The stuff your customers, your moms, and the world can see.) The list can include channels and tactics your company currently uses, or may use in the future. As participants call them out, draw a "ground line" half way down your white board and write their contributions above the line. (Clouds optional.)

ABOVE THE GROUND

P.R.
ADVERTISING SIGNAGE
EDUCATION & TRAINING
EMAIL
TRADE SHOWS
WEBSITE
SALES CALLS
SOCIAL MEDIA
SPONSORSHIPS

• After they have finished, add any above the ground tactics they forgot...newsletters, blogs, catalogs, etc. Explain that many if not all of these tactics will be re-crafted using the new Brand Promise, the three Support Pillars, and the Hero Statement.

• Next, explain before the world sees your new branding and marketing, "below the ground" integration must take place. This is the focus of today's Brainstorm Session. "Below the ground" elements are the behind-the-scenes underpinnings of your organization.

• Ask your group to call out their "below the ground" departments or business units. When they have finished add whatever you feel they missed.

• Now share this important marketing secret; The Brand Promise and Support Pillars that are reflected in the "below the ground" stuff—the important work they do every day, impacts business more than buying a Super Bowl TV commercial. Effective marketing is more about what you DO than what you SAY.

Inside scoop: The next exercise will cause three minutes of total chaos. As you run through the steps, even the most intelligent adults will become helpless children. Some will lash out. Others will retreat to a state of catatonia. Be strong.

• Inform your group this exercise requires them to split into three cohorts of a fairly equal number of people, e.g., 20 people will form cohorts of seven and seven and six.

 • Next, assign a roughly equal number of "below the ground" business units to each cohort. For instance, Cohort One will be brainstorming on Manufacturing, HR and Accounting. Cohort Two will brainstorm Advertising, Customer Support, IT. And Cohort Three will brainstorm Sales, Purchasing, Logistics and R&D. If possible, each cohort should include leadership from their assigned "below the ground" business units. To make this clear, go back to your white board and get visual.

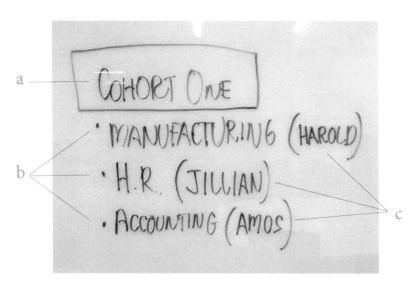

a — COHORT ONE

• MANUFACTURING (HAROLD)

b — • H.R. (JILLIAN)

• ACCOUNTING (AMOS) — c

On the white board: a) Number each of the cohorts. b) List the business units each cohort will be brainstorming. c) Write the names of each business unit leader. At this point all three cohorts include a business unit leader. The remaining participants should fill out the cohorts based on their interests or involvement in the company. You may have to reassign a few people to balance out the number of participants in each group. It's not ideal, but it's okay if cohorts include some participants whose area of expertise does not include the business units they will be brainstorming.

• Ask a volunteer from each cohort to record their group's ideas during the exercise, and be willing to report the best ones to the larger group afterwards.

• Refer to the PILLARS you posted on the wall as you explain these brainstorming steps.

• In a moment, each cohort will go to a corner of the large room, or to separate rooms if available. And in 5 minutes sprints, brainstorm new and better ways to implement SUPPORT PILLAR ONE to each of their assigned "below the ground" business units. In other words, during the first 5 minutes Cohort One will explore ways INNOVATIVE TECHNOLOGY could improve your MANUFACTURING processes. During the next 5 minutes Cohort One will explore ways INNOVATIVE TECHNOLOGY could improve your HUMAN RESOURCES department. And finally, they will explore ways INNOVATIVE TECHNOLOGY could improve your company's ACCOUNTING processes.

• Let them know you will alert everyone when each 5 minute sprint is over and they should move onto the next business unit. When they've brainstormed all business units under PILLAR ONE, they will repeat the exercise with PILLAR TWO and PILLAR THREE.

Here's a chart highlighting Cohort One's first 5 minute sprint.

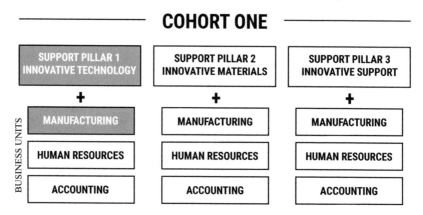

In this example, Cohort One will brainstorm 9 sprints for a total of 45 minutes. Cohorts with an extra business unit will need more time to complete their exercise.

• After all the cohorts have completed their sprints, give them 5 additional minutes to choose the best single idea per sprint they wish to share with the larger group.

• When all cohorts have chosen their best ideas, reconvene in the large room to share and discuss them.

• Have each representative read the best single idea per sprint to the larger group. It should go something like this:

COHORT ONE REPRESENTATIVE— *"Our first business unit is Manufacturing. Relative to Pillar One, Innovative Technology, we thought GPS technology would prevent accidents when moving large equipment from production line A to production line B. Our next business unit is HR. Bob suggested Innovative Technology like online tutorials and quizzes would speed up the on-boarding process. Lastly, under Pillar One, Sarah was really excited to suggest we use Innovative Technology in her accounting department to mitigate cyber security risks. In fact, she's already been looking at security platforms that protect customer and financial data as well as operational risks."*

• Ask each cohort to leave the notes holding all their ideas for future consideration.

• Wrap up the brainstorm session with these three achievements:

1) "Today, with your help, we validated some important work done by our marketing advisory committee; our PILLARS of Innovative technology, Innovative Materials and Innovative Support are three things that will benefit our customers, and when combined, differentiate our brand from everyone else out there."

2) "Today we achieved something most brands—especially B2B brands—don't or can't. Brand clarity. Yesterday if I asked 10 of you what makes our brand special or unique, I'd probably get 10 different answers. They may all be good, but different definitions confuse prospects. Today, everyone in this room knows that INNOVATION is what sets our brand apart."

3) "And last but not least, today we collected some amazing ideas on how to take our PILLARS—the things we're already good at and known for, and make them even more a part of who we are and how they improve our customers' lives."

• Ask the group to give it up for the cohort representatives and collect all of the brainstorm ideas for future consideration.

• Take a cleansing breath. You did it!

CHAPTER TWELVE

BRANDED MOMENTS – YOUR SECRET COMPETITIVE ADVANTAGE

On a pea soup-humid Florida night, my wife and two young kids checked into a hotel on the property of Walt Disney World. Exhausted from a long day of travel, we quickly unpacked. The kids put on their Mickey Mouse and 101 Dalmatians pajamas. I called the front desk for a 7:00 wake-up call (smart phones hadn't been invented yet) and we hit the pillows. At exactly 7:00 a.m. our room phone rang. In a daze I picked it up and held it to my ear. But instead of the recorded voice of a pleasant receptionist, it was Goofy's voice telling me, "It's time to jump outta bed and have yerself a Goofy day!" I was instantly charmed and hung up the phone laughing.

I'm sure Disney World ran ads (Branded Messaging) that reflected their Brand Pillar of FAMILY FUN, but I couldn't describe one advertisement to you now. What I do remember is the Branded *Moment* they provided. And that was over thirty years ago!

Around 1990, Lexus disrupted the luxury auto market in the United States. In those days, Cadillac, Audi, Lincoln, Porsche and Mercedes Benz were duking it out on TV and in magazines. Lexus joined the fight in Branded Messaging, too, but they used another tactic that put them in the passing lane: Brand Moments that supported their Pillar of REMARKABLE CUSTOMER CARE. When the proud owner of a shiny, new Lexus drove off the dealer lot, to her delight, her favorite stations were already programmed into the radio! How could that be? When she traded in her old car, the Lexus technician simply took note of the stations she had pre-set, and plugged the same ones into her new car radio. Lexus could have run an ad about their remarkable customer care. But a Branded Moment made it real, personal, memorable and remarkable.

Hospitals run ads about how much they care. (Virtually none of them work.) Let me share a little Branded Moment I overheard a few years ago that convinced me Fairview Southdale Hospital really does care a bit more than the rest.

I was visiting a sick friend when a nurse entered the room and asked me step out for a minute so he could examine his patient. While I waited outside I overheard a conversation between a hospital aid and an elderly patient. She explained (loudly, because of his poor hearing) that she was going to change his bed sheets while he was in the bed. Her directions were clear and compassionate but what happened next brought me to tears. She asked the old man if she could sing to him as they worked together to freshen up his bed. For just a minute or two I overheard the sweet chorus from "You are my sunshine." An uncomfortable, if not painful task for this patient, was transformed into a caring and comforting Branded Moment.

Branded Moments allow you to compete against—no, wait, BLOW AWAY your competitors without outspending them. Disney already owned the voice of Goofy, so there was no additional cost to create a fun and memorable "moment." Lexus invested three minutes to pre-program a radio before their car rolled off the lot. And in return, new owners felt pampered and excited to tell others about their experience. Fairview Southdale Hospital aids sing a song or tell a joke-of-the-day and LIVE their promise of care, rather than advertise it.

Special moments are nice. Lots of brands create special moments. But *Branded* Moments are special AND intrinsically tied to your brand and what it stands for. Let's generate some Branded Moments for your customers.

BRAINSTORM SESSION FOUR

CREATING BRANDED MOMENTS

60 MINUTES.

OBJECTIVE: Learn to create Branded Moments that can help your brand rise above your competition (Many for very little moola.)

DIRECTIONS: Over the next hour, your advisory committee will generate Branded Moments that will be captivating, memorable and talked about. This session requires a large conference room, a white board, and if possible, 3 small breakout rooms.

Because your Pillars support a bold promise and differentiate your brand, we'll be using your them as building blocks for brainstorming your Branded Moments.

There are several stages of customer engagement but for this Brainstorm Session we will focus on three:

1) Pre-engagement—before a prospect has made a purchase. At this stage they may or may not be engaged with your brand.

2) Engagement—the period in which customers are actively involved with your brand and/or using your products or services.

3) Post-engagement—your customer's life after the sale.

I'll use XYZ TrenchCo as a sample brand throughout the explanation.

• As shown on the opposite page, post your Brand Pillars in a single column. (Print them up ahead of time or mark them on the white board.)

• Read aloud each Pillar.

• Next, explain the three customer stages of engagement and create another column as shown.

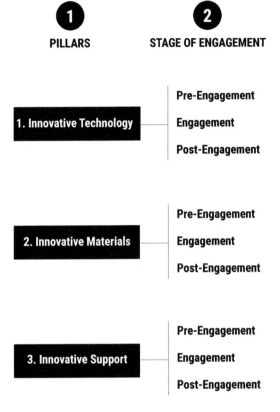

PILLARS	STAGE OF ENGAGEMENT	BRANDED MOMENTS
1	2	3

1. Innovative Technology
- Pre-Engagement
- Engagement
- Post-Engagement

2. Innovative Materials
- Pre-Engagement
- Engagement
- Post-Engagement

3. Innovative Support
- Pre-Engagement
- Engagement
- Post-Engagement

• Divide your group into three cohorts of an equal (or fairly equal) number of participants.

• Have them elect a spokesperson to write down and report the ideas to the larger group later.

• Assign one Pillar to each cohort. Over the next 45 minutes, your cohorts will scurry away to another room and brainstorm Branded Moments that reflect their assigned Pillar relative to each of the three customer stages of engagement. Creative sparks will be flying so be sure a fire extinguisher is located in each room.

• Alert them every 15 minutes to move onto the next stage of engagement until they have brainstormed all three.

• When the cohorts have finished, reconvene in the larger room and ask each cohort's spokesperson to read the best 1-2 ideas per engagement stage. Here are some XYZ TrenchCo examples:

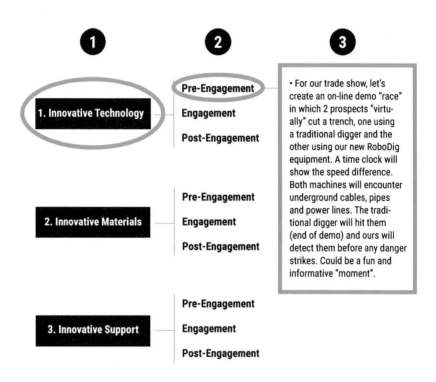

The Pillar of Innovative Technology applied to the Pre-Engagement stage of the customer journey (meaning, not yet a customer) led to an idea about a cool trade show demo.

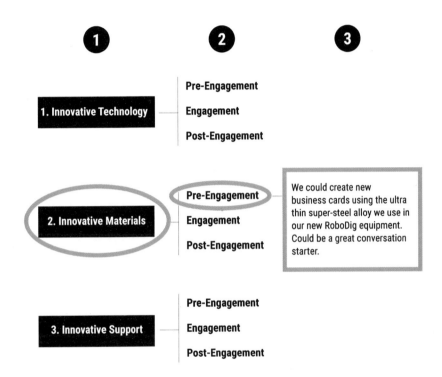

The Pillar of Innovative Materials applied to the Pre-Engagement stage of the customer journey (meaning, not yet a customer) led to an idea about a business card that would almost force the prospect to ask about the cool material it's made from.

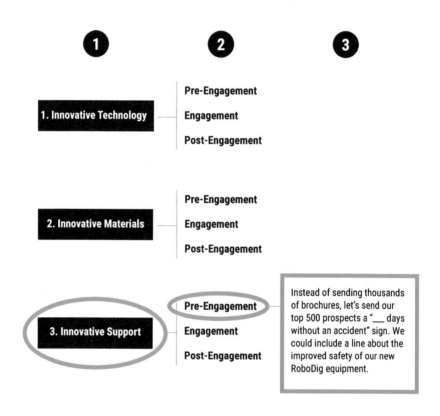

The Pillar of Innovative Support applied to the Pre-Engagement stage of the customer journey (meaning, not yet a customer) led to a valuable give away that supports the brand promise of safety.

Inside scoop: The best way to explain to your advisory committee what you are asking for is to give them a PILLAR + STAGE OF ENGAGEMENT = BRANDED MOMENT example. You could use the XYZ TrenchCo examples shown, or brainstorm a few on your own ahead of the session. Also, if your group is energized and feeling creative, loosen up on my time parameters and let them keep going.

• As a group, discuss the ideas and allow participants to build on them. Some of the ideas will be simply nice gestures like giving away branded pens, stress balls and other crap you see at trade shows. Nudge them toward ideas that reflect intrinsic aspects of your brand and your Brand Pillars.

Branded Moments are your secret weapon. Most require less money than any of the tactics in your media plan. Some will require no money at all. From now on, you'll have the one-two punch of Branded Messaging that gets traction and Branded Moments that create positive memories. How cool is that?

ROB POV

DOING THE RIGHT THINGS FOR THE WRONG REASONS.

Your job is to feed the marketing messages that work and starve the ones that do not. But be aware of customers who do the right thing (buy your products and services) but for the wrong reason (a benefit you don't promote).

I'd like to say I drive the speed limit because it's the responsible thing to do. Saving lives and all that. But the reality is, I drive the speed limit to avoid speeding tickets. Should my motive to comply to the posted speed limits matter to our highway patrol officers? Not as long as I comply. The hot water heaters ABC company manufactures will save home owners 10 % on their energy bills. This is a benefit they promote. But ABC's contractor customers may actually be specifying their brand because the water heaters take a few less minutes to install (a benefit ABC didn't feel was big enough to mention in their marketing.) So, stay in touch with your customers. You may learn they are buying your products for the wrong reasons. And those wrong reasons may lead to your next successful marketing campaign.

CHAPTER THIRTEEN

HOW TO LOSE CUSTOMERS (THE RIGHT WAY)

This book is for marketers who want to attract prospects and retain customers. I want to dedicate a few pages to talk about how to lose business, but lose it the "right" way.

Before I launch into this subject I must make a confession. In my younger years I did not always detach from employment positions, projects and business relationships the "right" way. A strong sense of competition and a dose of self-righteousness and immaturity sometimes prevented me from separating in a manner that was consistent with my values. (How's that for a fancy-schmancy way of saying I could be an a-hole?) But over time I came to realize, It's not how you start a relationship, but how you leave one that reflects your true character.

You made a thoughtful declaration when you created your brand values: the guiding principles all employees would live by. When you've been judged unfairly or fallen victim to uncontrollable circumstances that resulted in the loss of business you have a choice to make. And that choice will either give you a moment of satisfaction ("Oh, yeah? Well you can take this job and shove it"). Or, you can abide by your brand values and separate with professionalism and class. The second choice takes discipline, but it can pay long-term dividends. A couple stories to illustrate my point.

After a decade of serving our client, Boston Scientific, the company decided to move all of their marketing to Hill Holliday, an ad agency in Boston, MA. The decision had nothing to do with my ad agency's performance, but terminating our relationship simply made economic sense for our client. This was one of our biggest, blue chip accounts and could have been grounds for layoffs and deep operational cuts. By this time in my career I had learned to slow down and not react when bad news came our way. Instead, I knew to rely on our brand values of honesty, integrity and collaboration to guide my response. After my client finished her carefully worded "Dear John" phone call, my response was something like, "Sharon, we've worked together for ten years and I can't imagine how difficult this call is for you. How can we help you transition to your new agency?" By leaning on our brand values rather than my emotions, a remarkable thing happened. Sharon took us up on my offer. While the account did, in fact, move to the Boston agency, small projects were awarded to us over the course of several months. This gave us enough time and income to replace the account and avert layoffs, heartache and woe.

I relayed this story to a young marketing guy who I'll call Mike. (Because his name is Mike). One day Mike learned his entire marketing department was closing. At this point in his life a layoff was a terrible blow. Mike and his wife had recently purchased their first home and their first baby was on the verge of crowning. But Mike remembered my story about losing the Boston Scientific account. During his exit meeting, he asked how he could help management close the department and transition the workload to external vendors.

That day, every marketing department employee except one boxed up their coffee mugs, staplers and bobble-heads and left the building. Except one. Mike was invited to stay and help with the transition, giving him enough time to make a few mortgage payments, land the marketing job of his dreams and stay married.

So, how do you leave the "right" way when you are the party initiating the split? You rely on your brand values instead of your emotions. (Sound familiar?)

My ad agency won a small assignment from a building

materials manufacturer. The results of that project brought triple the desired response and within a few weeks the manufacturer invited us to become their agency of record. Thirteen projects came in the door on Day One of our official relationship. But along with a workload that would have nearly doubled our revenues, came the instructions my business partner and I could not accept. The company owner would be the decision maker for all of our advertising and marketing work, but we were not allowed to speak directly to him. On the morning of Day Two, Keith Sherman (my then business partner) called the manufacturer and resigned the business. He explained that our company was about integrity and collaboration. And that collaboration didn't just mean we were communicative, but that we rolled up our sleeves and worked shoulder to shoulder with the people who would ultimately approve our strategies and ideas. He went on to explain our experience had shown us, without access to the decision makers, advertising concepts miss the mark, approval takes twice as long and agency/client relationships wither and die.

Within 24 hours of that call, three of the company's four marketing directors contacted us and in hushed voices, commended us on our brave decision to resign their business. They admitted they had previously burned through several ad agencies because of their flawed protocol, and they wished us well.

But it gets better. The story of how we resigned that piece of business was passed from one of those marketing directors to a trusted media rep. The media rep was impressed and he recommended our firm to the marketing director of a different building materials manufacturer who called us, hired us and became one of our most profitable and fun accounts.

This is not an unusual story. Over the course of ten years, my advertising agency chose not to pursue at least 30% of the opportunities that came our way because they did not allow us to live our brand values. Those clients who shared our values were a great fit for us.

Closing doors the "right" way often opens others. Integrity and high standards means something in this world. Losing customers the right way is good for the soul. And it turns out, it's good for business, too.

Thank you for entrusting me to help you power up your B2B branding. Marketing is fun. Especially when you do your homework, use proven processes, and have the tools and confidence to disrupt the marketplace and grow your business. Now get out there and take charge!

ACKNOWLEDGEMENTS

It's called source amnesia. You know a fact but you can't, for the life of you, recall where or from whom you learned it. (I know that a stalk of sweet corn will produce two ears but I can't tell you who told me this.) I want to acknowledge the people who taught me so many of the ideas, practices and principles I discuss in this book. I want to thank my teachers, creative directors and clients who set incredibly high standards and demanded I rise to meet them. I want to give a shout out to the authors, bloggers and speakers who have inspired me to strive for greatness in every endeavor. And of course, thank my friends who have supported and encouraged me to be brave and act on my ideas. But, when I try to match up the information or inspiration to its source, with a few notable exceptions, my memory fails me. Those exceptions include Tom Blessing, my first mentor. Tom Wilson, who encouraged me not to "wait for a better time" when I was making plans to leave advertising and turn brand therapy into a full time gig. Sam Richter, who convinced me I could write the book I had hidden inside me. Tom McElligott who taught me how to work and work and work until the advertising I created *demanded* its intended audience stop in their tracks and pay attention. Hobart Stocking, Skip Zetzman, Cathy Brown, Dan Wallace, Paul Maccabee, Thom Winninger, Mariann Hohe, and so many others who fixed my typos, encouraged me and offered advice so generously. My son Alex and his wife Lindsay who constantly demonstrate the power of craft and genuine customer care as they grow their thriving business in Denver. My daughter (and Director of Google's Global Experience Strategy from the London office of Essence) Claire Grinton, who widens my marketing horizons every time we talk shop. Alex Grinton (Claire's husband and creative director at Anomaly/London) whose creativity, curiosity and disdain for all things formulaic is a constant inspiration. Okay, I'm proud of my kids and their spouses. Thanks for indulging me. And finally, an acknowledgement to my kind, generous, and all-around amazing wife, Debbie Dalton, who for over four decades, never doubted me. Well, maybe a little for my fashion sense.

To download the Dalton Brand Catalyst Toolkit, visit daltonbrandcatalyst.com. Password: WONDERPUP (All caps.)

If you'd like to chat with me about this book, your brand, or the marketing challenges and opportunities you are facing today, shoot me an email at rob@daltonbrandcatalyst.com.

Author Rob Dalton caught a lucky break starting his career at the time Minneapolis, Minnesota was emerging as the epicenter of advertising creativity. He worked for and with many of the industry's most brilliant marketers and ad creators at premiere agencies including Fallon and Martin Williams, eventually earning a reputation for creative excellence in his own right. His work has won awards in virtually every national advertising competition. Rob's roster of past clients include FedEx, Target, Lee Jeans, The Wall Street Journal, Delta Airlines, Ford Lincoln-Mercury, 3M, as well as several challenger brands including AmericInn Hotels, Dunn Bros Coffee, Super Clean, and more. Rob's Business To Business clients include Boston Scientific, Boeing, Fair Isaac & Company (FICO), Uponor, NextEra Analytics and dozens more, large and small.

Rob caught an even luckier break when he married his high school sweetheart in 1976. He and his wife Debbie raised two amazing kids who continue to delight and inspire them, even though they live much too far away.

Several years ago, one of Rob's clients referred to him as their "brand therapist" because of his nurturing processes and approachable demeanor. The title stuck.